50 GREATS
HEREFORD UNITED FOOTBALL CLUB

Best Wishes
David Edge. 15/9/06.

50 GREATS
HEREFORD UNITED FOOTBALL CLUB

DENISE POWELL & DAVE EDGE

TEMPUS

First published 2005

Tempus Publishing Limited
The Mill, Brimscombe Port,
Stroud, Gloucestershire, GL5 2QG
www.tempus-publishing.com

British Library Cataloguing in Publication Data.
A catalogue record for this book is available from the British Library.

ISBN 0 7524 3607 4

Typesetting and origination by Tempus Publishing Limited.
Printed in Great Britain.

Acknowledgements

We would like to thank Phill Gough, Carol Hopkins, Luke Powell, Tony Lerigo and Keith Lynham for their help, support, encouragement and interest as the book came together.

A deserved special mention goes to Jackie McKelvie, a football widow for over twenty years for her support of Hereford United FC.

Many thanks to the *Hereford Times*, especially Richard Prime, for the many photographs supplied and to the staff of Hereford United FC.

Ricky George (left) and Billy Meadows (right) with Victor Railton, chief football writer of *The London Evening News*, on the occasion of the 1972 FA Cup fifth round draw.

Foreword

This book has been ably compiled by two regular supporters of Hereford United, who, during many years of the existence of the Bulls, have travelled many miles, giving their support. I am sure that the book will be welcomed by the present and past fans of the club. Hereford United have been fortunate in having a good many coaching staff and scouts to bring some excellent players to Edgar Street and welded them into useful teams. Most, if not all, have been considered 'great' in their day, and it must have been a difficult task to chose fifty 'greats' out of the long list of 'greats' who have entertained so many supporters over the years. I have been lucky enough to see every one of the footballers included in this book play, and will appreciate the visit down memory lane! Enjoy your reading and memories.

Tony Lerigo
Lifelong fan of Hereford United

Hereford United *v.* West Ham United, Edgar Street, 1972. This FA Cup match finished in a 0-0 draw.

Introduction

If you asked fifty Hereford United fans to select the fifty greatest players to have represented the club you would undoubtedly get fifty different selections. While it is quite possible that the majority of players would be selected by all there is no doubt that there would be a number of individual and interesting selections. This would start a debate as to whether Steve White was a better striker than Dixie McNeil or if Tommy Hughes was a better goalkeeper than Fred Potter. Then the question as to whether John Charles was a better player at centre forward than centre half would be asked. Debates such as these often take place with fans of all football clubs, no matter which League they play in.

The selection found in this book includes such prolific goal scorers as Stewart Phillips and Steve White. Also included are former internationals such as Terry Paine, a member of the England World Cup-winning squad in 1966, and Adam Musial, who represented the club some years after being a member of the Poland team which finished third in West Germany in the 1974 World Cup. Representing Wales is another popular player, Brian Evans, who remains the only player to gain a full international cap while playing for the club. Early in 2004 Paul Parry gained the first of his Welsh caps just six weeks after leaving Hereford United.

Managers have come and gone but names such as John Sillett, Colin Addison and Graham Turner will always remain although only Colin Addison played for the club.

Hereford United *50 Greats* is intended to remind and inform fans of just some of the great players who have represented the club since it was formed in 1928. While whichever fifty chosen will not satisfy everyone, we hope that there is enough information in this book to bring back fond memories of players who were just of some of the great names of Hereford United FC.

Denise Powell and Dave Edge
October 2005

50 Hereford United Greats

Colin Addison
Tony Byrne
John Charles
Ray Daniel
Steve Davey
John Delve
Rob Elmes
Steve Emery
Brian Evans
John Galley
Ricky George
Bobby Gould
Harry Gregory
Roger Griffiths
Jimmy Harvey
Tommy Hughes
Peter Isaac
Tony James
Alan Jones
Alan Judge
Mick McLaughlin
Gavin Mahon
Dixie McNeil
Ken Mallender
Billy Meadows
Tamika Mkandawire
Adam Musial
Tommy Naylor
Brian Owen
Terry Paine
Paul Parry
Darren Peacock
Mel Pejic
Stewart Phillips
Jamie Pitman
Fred Potter
Chris Price
Ron Radford
Eric Redrobe
Steve Ritchie
David Rudge
Kevin Sheedy
Peter Spiring
Colin Tavener
Charlie Thompson
Peter Timms
Billy Tucker
Dudley Tyler
Joe Wade
Steve White

Note on Statistics

The authors have made every effort to ensure that player statistics are correct. However, discrepancies between sources may have resulted in some inaccuracies.

Colin Addison

Midfield, 1971–1974

Prior to 1972/73

	Appearances	Goals
	44	

Football League era

	Appearances	Goals
League	23	1
Other	2	

Previous clubs: York City, Nottingham Forest, Arsenal, Sheffield United

The 1971/72 season began brightly, but gave no clue as to what would unfold during the next twelve months. No doubt many fans were surprised when John Charles quit as manager early in the 1971/72 season to concentrate on his sports shop, but the replacement, Colin Addison, who was signed from Sheffield United as player-manager, proved to be a blessing in disguise. Hereford finished runners-up in the Southern League, reached the final of the Southern League Cup and were elected to the Football League in place of Barrow. The Bulls then finished runners-up to Southport in their first season in the Football League to gain promotion.

Colin Addison was born in Taunton in 1940 and later moved to York with his parents. He signed professional forms for York City on his seventeenth birthday in May 1957 and made his debut for the Bootham Crescent club in 1958, three years after joining them at the age of fifteen. He scored 27 goals in 87 League matches for York and in 1960 he was transferred to Nottingham Forest for £12,000, where he scored 61 goals in 159 League games. In September 1966 he moved to Arsenal for a £40,000 fee and two years later he was sold to Sheffield United for £45,000. Here Colin helped the Blades to win promotion to the First Division in the 1970/71 season. He played a total of 389 League games, scoring 120 goals.

The fee was a more modest £3,000 when Colin Addison transferred to Hereford as player-manager, and he made his Southern League debut against local rivals Worcester City at Edgar Street. Within a month of his arrival United had started on their unforgettable FA Cup run and this in turn helped United on their way to their debut in the Football League. Among his dislikes he lists losing and having to postpone games, a feature of the matches against Newcastle United in that cup run. His first instruction to the players at St James' Park for the first game against Newcastle was, 'You have earned the right to be here. Get out there and have a walk on the park. Get your heads up, look confident, you have a chance to show the world what you can do.' This phrase is the key to why teams from lower divisions give at least one stunning performance when confronted with top-class opposition. The

Manager Addison at his desk, 1972.

chance lets them prove to themselves and others how good they really are.

One of Colin's most memorable goals for Hereford United was at St James' Park. He took a pass from Ken Mallender minutes before half-time and moved forward into space. The Newcastle defenders backed off, marking the Hereford runners. Sensing his chance the player-manager shot from twenty-five yards, the ball never rising above knee height. McFaul, the Newcastle United goalkeeper, never moved.

On the day of the return match at Edgar Street, Addison pinned the photograph of Malcolm Macdonald holding up two hands, predicting a score of ten goals against Hereford, up on the dressing room wall as an incentive, in case one was needed! The 2-2 draw ensured United played a total of ten matches in the FA Cup that season and won the *Sunday Mirror* giant-killers award after beating Newcastle United and holding West Ham to a deserved draw. That season United finished runners-up in the Southern League but it was sufficient to earn them enough votes for election to the Football League. Colin's enthusiasm and ability to get the best out of his players helped United to finish runners-up in the Fourth Division at their first attempt. At the start of the season Colin was quoted as saying, 'We have to learn to walk before we can run. While our obvious aim will be to try to gain promotion in our first season in the League, it's no use building castles in the air. You can aim for the stars and set your standards high, but you have to be realistic about things in the end. We've had tremendous success in my short time with the club, and I'll never forget it. But I'm prepared to accept that there may be some dark days ahead too. Football's a life of ups and downs. When I first joined the club I said that I had no regrets about leaving the First Division. I haven't changed my mind.' After United won promotion at the first attempt, there were many tributes written to the Bulls and their young manager. The legendary John Charles said, 'Colin Addison has done a good job, and the team have done very well. All teams should have a similar chance to prove themselves. There should be some sort of automatic

The manager reads about his famous Giant-killing team.

progression from league to league.' Len Shipman was quoted as saying, 'I am delighted with Hereford's performance. They have shown that when clubs are given the chance they can prove worthy of the opportunity. Their new blood has been a good boost for football.' Dudley Tyler, who had made the move to West Ham, said, 'Hereford surprised everyone, including me, with their terrific run in the last half of the season. They proved just how much they deserved their place in the Football League.' There was similar praise from Sam Morgan, chairman of Barrow, who lost their League status to Hereford United: 'We hold no grudges against them. When they were elected into the League instead of us we sent them a letter of congratulations and wished them the best of luck. I am pleased to see they have done so well. They are having their success at the moment but their time to suffer will come. It's bound to, because soccer works in cycles, no-one can stay on top.' How prophetic that statement proved to be. Colin inspired loyalty from his players and created a superb team spirit within the football club. The following season saw Hereford United pulled out of the hat against West Ham United once again and, this time, the Bulls were the victors, after a replay. The manager later revealed that four key players (goalkeeper Tommy Hughes, striker

Eric Redrobe, defender Ron Radford and midfielder Colin Tavener) all played carrying injuries received at Upton Park. Unfortunately, Colin broke his leg in a match against in Barnsley in November 1972, but he made his comeback a year later in an FA Cup match against Torquay and played his final League match in March 1974. Colin left Hereford United in 1974 after a dispute and managed Durban City, a South African team, before becoming coach at Notts County. Colin was appointed manager of Newport County in February 1977 at a time when their fortunes had taken a turn for the worse. He was hailed as a miracle worker by the fans at Somerton Park after motivating the team and taking them from the bottom of the table, clear of the re-election zone. His progress was noted and in 1978 he was appointed assistant manager at West Bromwich Albion, Ron Atkinson being appointed as manager. In July 1979 Colin Addison was appointed manager of Derby County, who had narrowly avoided relegation a few months earlier. Although he was assisted by John Newman he failed to solve the problems at the Baseball Ground and, after slipping into the Second Division, it proved an uphill struggle trying to get them back into the top flight. After leaving Derby, Colin had a second spell at Newport County, again working wonders for the Welsh club, helping them avoid relegation, before almost achieving promotion the following season. He has also managed Spanish sides Celta Vigo and Atletico Madrid. He returned to Edgar Street for another season in 1990 and has more recently had spells in Spain, before returning to England to manage Forest Green Rovers, Scarborough, Yeovil and Barry Town. It was once said of Colin that he has been a great ambassador for the game and has always led by example, only asking of others what he has been prepared to do himself.

Colin was granted a benefit match by the directors of Newport County, but it ended up being played at Edgar Street. Ron Atkinson was in charge of Manchester United at the time and he agreed to bring a side to Somerton Park but UEFA and FIFA had banned English clubs from playing friendly matches in Wales, so the Hereford United board of directors stepped in and allowed the match to be played at Edgar Street. The majority of the Giant-killing XI returned to Edgar Street to play in the game, along with players who had played with Colin in the League at Edgar Street. Colin Addison has many fond memories of his time at Edgar Street and once said that the Hereford United supporters were worth another eleven players on the pitch. Their vocal encouragement was worth a goal start in every home game. Even though his career has taken him to many areas of the world his home has remained in Hereford and he even has a road named after him.

Tony Byrne

Defender, 1974–1977

Football League era

	Appearances	Goals
League	54 (1)	
Other	7	2

Previous clubs: Millwall, Southampton

Anthony Byrne, known to all Hereford United fans as Tony, was born in at Rathdowney, Eire, on 2 February 1946. He started his football career with League club Millwall in August 1963, but only made 1 appearance for the London club before he moved on a year later to join Southampton. Between 1966 and 1973 the defender made 81 full appearances for the club and was a substitute on 14 occasions, scoring 3 goals. During that time he represented the Eire international team, gaining 14 caps. His caps came in a four-year period as the Republic of Ireland slowly but surely developed into a force in world football. One of his caps was against Poland in a friendly international at Lansdowne Road, Dublin, in October 1973, when another future Hereford United player, Adam Musial, lined up for the opposition. Eire won 1-0, which was a feather in the cap for fans and country alike as the previous Wednesday Poland had qualified for the World Cup finals in Germany at the expense of both England and Wales. Joining Hereford in August 1974 for an £18,000 transfer fee, he made his League debut in the first home game of the season against Aldershot. He missed only one League match that season as the club, by now under the control of John Sillett, finished a respectable twelfth. Although Tony worked tirelessly defending the Hereford goal, his efforts in helping the attack were unrewarded and he failed to get his name on the scoresheet during a League game. The following season he only made one full League appearance for the club, on 25 October 1975. Although Hereford lost a memorable encounter 2-4 at home to Peterborough that day, the match is often remembered as the day Terry Paine celebrated his 765th League appearance. However, Tony made a number of appearances for Hereford in the Welsh Cup that season as Hereford progressed to the final. He was also more successful in front of goal for the club in this competition, scoring in both the semi-final against Shrewsbury Town and the final against Cardiff City. His goal in the ninetieth minute against Shrewsbury Town, away from home, rescued United, who were losing 2-1 on aggregate. Steve Davey had taken the ball past three men for Tony to score with the last kick of the match. With no more goals in extra time the match went to penalties, but United won

Tony Byrne in action.

5-4 to go through to the final. Sadly they lost 6-5 on aggregate in the two-legged final, with Tony scoring his goal away from home in the second leg. Steve Davey had a header in the last minute that beat the goalkeeper but unluckily for Hereford the ball stuck in the mud. During the club's only season in the Second Division Tony Byrne made eight League appearances before leaving in March 1977 to join Newport County. While at Somerton Park he made 80 appearances in Newport colours, scoring once. After leaving Newport and League football Tony played non-League football for a number of years; his clubs included Trowbridge Town, Ledbury Town and Dales United. Later he moved into football management, managing local clubs in the Herefordshire Football League.

John Charles

Centre forward/centre half, 1966–1971

Prior to 1972/73

Appearances	Goals
243	130

Previous clubs: Leeds United, Juventus, Roma, Cardiff City

There are many Hereford United fans who consider the signing of John Charles, who was arguably the greatest player of his generation and who had the unique ability to play at centre half or centre forward, to be the best ever made by the club. John Charles played at the highest level, which included the 1958 World Cup in Sweden with Wales. He played for Leeds United, Juventus, Roma and Cardiff City before joining Hereford United as a player, and he eventually became player-manager, succeeding Bob Dennison. The inspirational figure on the football field now became the inspirational manager who started the rise of the club towards its glory days of the 1970s.

John Charles was once described as the best centre forward and centre half in the world at the same time. His performances for the Turin giants Juventus won him almost divine status in Italy. He was known as *il Gigante Buono* ('the Gentle Giant'). Big John was born in Swansea in December 1931, signed for Leeds United in January 1949 at the age of seventeen and gained the first of his 38 international caps for Wales shortly after his eighteenth birthday. His schoolmasters at Swansea had tipped John to become a Test cricketer but he chose football as his career, and what an illustrious career it was. Yet he could also have been a boxer, having demolished a string of opponents as a heavyweight fighter while a national serviceman. He made his debut for Leeds United against Scottish club Queen of the South. in a friendly He was just seventeen when he was called upon by Major Frank Buckley, the manager of Leeds, to walk from his place at centre half to the penalty spot to take a penalty in the middle of a crowd riot at Plymouth. With the coolness of a ten-year veteran he scored and showed that there was a promising career ahead. His 42 goals in the Second Division in the 1953/54 season were a club record for Leeds United. The following season he scored 30 goals as Leeds won promotion to the First Division. Even in the First Division the goals continued to flow; his

The famous man in action for Hereford United.

38 goals in the 1956/57 season made him the Football League's top scorer. After scoring 151 goals for Leeds, John Charles left Elland Road for Juventus in 1957, for the record-breaking fee of £65,000. He was one of the first British players to be successful playing in Italy and was eventually voted the greatest foreign player ever in Serie A, putting him above Diego Maradona, Michel Platini and Zinedine Zidane. After a brief return to Leeds in the early 1960s, John Charles returned to Italy to play for Roma for a fee of £70,000, before returning to Britain in August 1963. He played for Cardiff City for two seasons, scoring 19 goals in 66 appearances for the Bluebirds.

John Charles' international career lasted fifteen years. His first international was against Northern Ireland in 1950 when he played centre half in a goal-less draw. He helped Wales reach the quarter-finals of the World Cup in 1958 in Sweden. An injury in the 2-1 win over Hungary prevented him playing, however, in the narrow 1-0 defeat by Brazil, the eventual winners of the World Cup. His final international game was against the USSR in Moscow in May 1965. The majority of his international appearances were as a defender but John still managed to score 15 goals in his 38 appearances for Wales.

The only time that John Charles ever showed signs of losing his temper was when Wales were playing Austria and an opponent tackled his younger brother Mel. He was a scrupulously fair competitor who detested dirty play and his anger only surfaced if he sensed injustice.

John Charles signed for Hereford United in the summer of 1966 and took over as player-manager in 1967 when Bob Dennison left to become chief scout for Coventry City. John scored on his debut, early in the second half in a 5-1 victory over Bedford. Soon after his arrival at Edgar Street the former England winger Eddie Holliday was also brought to United to provide service to Big John and in his first 24 games John Charles scored 25 goals. He admitted to 'still getting a hell of a kick at seeing the ball go in the net'. For away fixtures every club would ring up to make sure that John Charles was playing because of the interest that he created and the extra crowds who would attend. Indeed, he was thanked by Nuneaton Borough because their takings were the highest for eleven years, some £700. Things went so well for John at Edgar Street that Bury of the Second Division, and also an Italian club, asked him to join them, but John refused because he was happy where he was. He made 243 first-team appearances for United, scoring 130 goals, with over 100 scored at Edgar Street. Big John scored five goals in a match against Folkestone Town in 1966/67 and four goals against each of Chelmsford City and Newport County in a Southern League match and Herefordshire Senior Cup match respectively in the same week. He also scored Hereford United's only goal in the 1967/68 Welsh Cup final against Cardiff City. In the second round of the FA Cup on 6 January 1968 Hereford United were drawn against Watford at Vicarage Road and, just before the interval, John Charles broke his nose in a collision, but he carried on playing until the final whistle. One of John Charles's most famous goals was the one he scored against Brighton & Hove Albion on 12 December 1970 in the FA Cup second round. His ability to lift his large frame a metre off the ground and hover was legendary, and the Seagulls' goalkeeper was well beaten by his thundering header. He resigned in October 1971 but continued his playing career with Merthyr Tydfil. During his time at Edgar Street he had helped United through a bad financial spell and had brought the club to the forefront of non-League football. The average gate had risen to 5,000, better than that of many League clubs. He had also brought to Edgar Street many of the players who were destined to become members of the famous 'Giant-killing' team. He delighted all the team when he appeared in the dressing room after the memorable victory over Newcastle United, such was his charisma.

Opposing players said that he was impossible to mark, particularly at set pieces. There are stories from his time in Italy that opponents would be literally hanging onto him with arms around his waist as corners came over. 'Charlo' would simply shrug them off and plant the header wherever he felt that it should go. It wasn't his height; although an advantage, it was his timing, which was immaculate. He could hang in the air, it seemed, for as long as he wanted. Michael Parkinson described the way he hovered in the air as looking like an eagle among sparrows, a predator surveying lunch.

He was an impressive-looking man, six feet three inches tall, fourteen stone, with the physique of an Ancient Greek athlete; a square chin, straight nose and a permanent suntan. A big man with very few words to say, his team talks were legendary – sometimes there just weren't any. To be so famous yet so completely unassuming was his greatest asset. He never turned his physique to unfair advantage. People often claimed he could have crushed lighter opponents on the football pitch. He had the ability to make fifty-yard bursts that threw defences into panic and hit some of the most breathtaking shots never before seen.

He was also described as the complete footballer and was a member of the 'Goaldiggers', a charity organisation that raised money to develop play areas for youngsters.

Sadly, John Charles developed Alzheimer's, but not before his autobiography had been written. When he came to a Hereford bookshop to sign copies a long queue developed. Everyone wanted a copy signed, young and old, such was his popularity and he had the time to smile for one and all, whether he knew them or not. Other illnesses followed and the Gentle Giant passed away in February 2004.

Ray Daniel

Midfield, 1960–1967

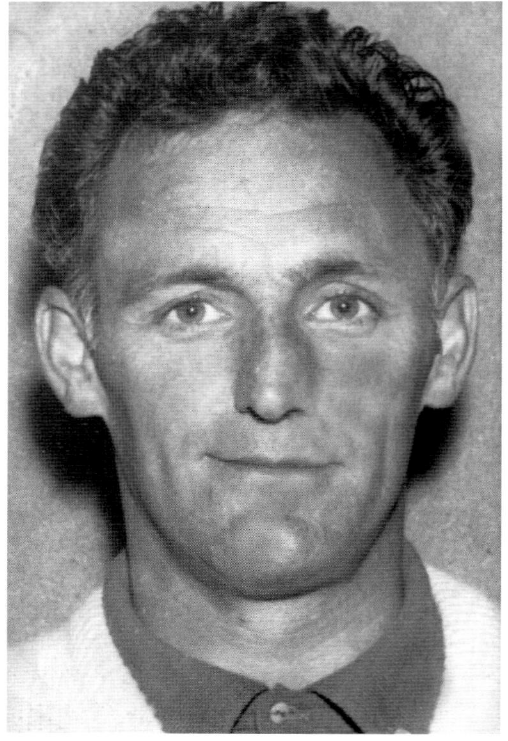

Prior to 1972/73

	Appearances	Goals
	317	66

Previous clubs: Swansea Town, Arsenal, Sunderland, Cardiff City, Swansea

Ray W. Daniel was born in Swansea in November 1928 and was signed as an amateur by his home-town football club Swansea Town, as they were known then. His unique style of football soon attracted the attention of the bigger clubs and he signed for Arsenal in October 1946. He played a total of 87 matches for the Gunners during the four seasons he was with them. He played as centre half in the FA Cup final against Newcastle United at Wembley, which they lost 1-0 in 1952. Arsenal had been reduced to playing with ten men after full-back Walley Barnes badly injured a knee. Ray also played the whole of the match with a broken wrist, which was set in a cast. Other Arsenal injuries included Doug Lishman, who had a septic cut, and Jimmy Logie, who had an internal haemorrhage. Daniel described the cup final as the best match that skipper Joe Mercer ever played in. Ray's job was to mark Jackie Milburn out of the game. During his time at Arsenal, Daniel was also capped by Wales Under-21s and became a full international on 15 November 1950 in a match against England at Roker Park, which England won 4-2. In all, Ray was capped 21 times by Wales, the final match being against Czechoslovakia in Prague in 1957.

Ray Daniel played for Wales at a time when they did not have a lot of money – everything was done on a shoestring! All they had was the basic strip of shorts, shirts and socks. The players had to take along everything else, including soap and a towel for the bath. Usually the squad was no larger than fourteen, but there was often double that number of officials in the party! On one occasion, one of the players was left off the plane to France because there were not enough seats. Not one of the non-playing officials offered to give up their seat and the player had to wait for the next plane to join the team. Ray was called up late to join the Welsh squad, after injury and illness within the squad, for the match against Czechoslovakia. Sunderland sent a new pair of football boots to the airport for him instead of his old ones. After training all day in the new boots, Ray's feet were blistered, and he tried a pair of John Charles's but they did not fit. Emil Zatopek, a runner, who was staying at the same hotel, made some pads to fit inside the boots to try to ease the pain. Unfortunately Ray Daniel scored an own goal and Wales lost 2-0, Ray was in so much pain that he kicked off his boots fifteen minutes before the end of the game and played the remainder in his socks! Ray was not dropped from the Welsh squad because of the own goal – the story has it that it was for singing songs from West End shows that were considered risqué by some religious members of the international committee. In 1951 Ray was also selected as a member of the Wales side who beat a Rest of the United Kingdom XI 3-2 at Ninian Park. A transfer in June 1953 took Ray Daniel to Roker Park after he signed a contract for Sunderland. He made 137 League appearances in four seasons, scoring 6 goals. In October 1957 he moved to Cardiff City but made just 6 appearances before being signed by Swansea twelve weeks later. After making 44 appearances for Swansea and scoring 6 goals, Ray Daniel was signed by Hereford United at the start of the 1960/61 season, at the same time as goalkeeper Peter Isaac. Joe Wade, the former Arsenal colleague of Ray Daniel, was manager of the Bulls at the time. To start with, Daniel played as centre forward for Hereford United and in his first season he scored hat-tricks in the Southern League matches against Gravesend, both home and away. He was a member of the team that gained a great replay in the FA Cup in the 1961/62 season against Bristol City after a 1-1 draw away. A rugged and determined Hereford United team of heroes, which included Peter Isaac in goal and centre half Ray Daniel, kept Bristol City at bay and proved themselves equal to their full-time League opposition. Over 2,000 Bulls supporters made the trip to Bristol by trains, cars and coaches. United put up a splendid display against a side fifth in the Third Division and who had been beaten only once in their previous nine matches. A crowd of over 11,000 packed into United's ground at Edgar Street to see the replay, hoping to see a giant-killing, but it was not to be. Despite Ray Daniel scoring from the penalty spot Bristol City scored twice in the last quarter of an hour to end up convincing winners, even if the scoreline of 5-2 slightly flattered them. The consolation for United was that the club finances had been boosted by over £1,500 from the two fixtures that had attracted a combined gate of 25,640 football fans.

Joe Wade resigned in 1962 to concentrate on his sports shop in Hereford and Ray Daniel was appointed player-manager. While manager, Hereford United reached the first round of the FA Cup once more and this time they played Crystal Palace at Selhurst Park in front of a crowd of 15,317 but, despite fine performances from Ray Daniel and goalkeeper Peter Isaac, the Glaziers won 2-0. Hereford United also reached the semi-final of the Welsh Cup that season, losing 1-0 to Borough United who went on to win the final. At that time there were no rules to stop an English club winning the trophy and going on to play in the European Cup-Winners' Cup, although by the time Hereford United won the trophy the rule had changed to stop this from happening. Borough United beat Sliema Wanderers in Europe before going out to Slovan Bratislava. Unfortunately he was not rated as a successful manager, and Ray Daniel was eventually succeeded by Bob Dennison halfway through the following season. Ray stayed with the Bulls as a player and when he finally retired from playing football he had made 317 first-team appearances and scored 66 goals. Ray Daniel was once described as 'an extrovert veteran' who once claimed to have been dazzled by the floodlights when scoring an own goal!

Steve Davey

Striker, 1975–1978

Steve Davey was a footballer whose pace and fitness earned him many fans in the south of the country and here in the Midlands, with spells at Plymouth Argyle, Hereford United, Portsmouth and Exeter City. He was born in Plymouth on 5 September 1948 and was signed up by his home-town club as an apprentice in July 1966 after leaving school. His talent was quickly noticed and he almost immediately gained England Youth honours in 1967. In his seven full seasons with the Home Park club Steve made 226 League appearances and scored 48 goals. He was often given a supporting striking role and many of his goals were scored as a result of his sharpness over the first six yards, when he usually out-paced the defender marking him. Probably his best season for Argyle was 1973/74 when he was their top scorer. He scored seven goals in the League Cup as his team went on to reach the semi-finals.

In June 1975 Hereford United's manager John Sillett (who can list Plymouth Argyle as one of his previous clubs) put in an offer of £6,500 for Steve but this was rejected by Argyle. Sillett did not give up, realising Steve had great potential, and kept up the pressure until an increased fee of £9,000 was agreed between the two clubs. Steve went on to miss just one League game in the Third Division championship-winning season. He was second-top scorer behind Dixie McNeil – in fact their devastatingly effective partnership was the best in the Football League that season. Steve made his League debut for the Bulls on 16 August 1975 in a goal-less draw with Port Vale, but the Bulls fans did not have long to wait for the goals to start. His first goal came in a 1-1 draw at home to Gillingham and he then went on to score in each of the next two games, which resulted in victories over Chester and Wrexham. Although Steve Davey was not as prolific a goal-scorer as Dixie, the two complemented each other and their partnership was the best that United had enjoyed since their admission to the Football League. Steve Davey was instrumental in United's success, very often latching on to passes from Terry Paine, and then

Football League era

	Appearances	Goals
League	104 (3)	32
Other	16 (1)	2

Previous clubs: Plymouth Argyle

feeding the ball through to Dixie for him to go and score past the opposition. In all Steve scored 18 League goals that season, probably none more important to him than the brace scored against Gillingham away from home. The first goal came within two minutes of the kick-off, Steve nodding Dixie's cross in off the post. Gillingham replied with two goals, and unhappily for the United fans Steve Ritchie scored an own goal to put them 3-1 up. The Hereford United team then showed all the qualities that were to take them to the top of the League, by battling back to a 4-3 victory with another goal from Steve Davey and goals from Dixie and John Layton. Steve's second goal came from a neat move involving John Galley and Lindsay. Between them all they earned a standing ovation from the near-8,000 crowd, and their twelfth away win opened up a seven-point gap at the top of the table.

Steve made 21 appearances in Hereford United's season in the Second Division and was again second-top scorer with 9 goals, behind Dixie McNeil. Their striking partnership managed twenty-five goals but unfortunately it was not enough to keep them in that League and relegation followed back to the Third Division. Steve managed a brace at Eastville, home of

Davey heads for goal, *c.* 1976.

Bristol Rovers, in a 3-2 victory and in a 3-3 draw with Bolton Wanderers at Edgar Street. He also scored a goal against his old club Plymouth Argyle in April 1977. The following season saw his striking partner Dixie transferred to Wrexham for mainly financial reasons; the club had been living beyond its means. Victories were far and few between and the fact that Steve Davey was joint-top scorer with only 5 League goals told its own story.

In his three seasons with the Bulls Steve made over 100 appearances and scored 32 goals, and in June 1978 he was transferred to Portsmouth for £10,000, again as a cost-cutting measure. Here, Steve again made over 100 appearances before transferring to Exeter City where he ended his illustrious Football League career. He later returned to Plymouth Argyle to help with coaching where his son was a YTS trainee. He retained his links with United and suggested a number of players for trials. It was Steve that encouraged United to sign Owen Pickard, who was to become the club's top scorer. Hereford United fans will long remember Steve for his pace, crisp passing and eye for goal, and his prolific partnership with Dixie.

John Delve

Midfield, 1983–1987

Football League era

	Appearances	Goals
League	116 (2)	11
Other	11	1

Previous clubs: Queens Park Rangers, Plymouth Argyle, Exeter City

John Delve first came to Edgar Street in September 1974, as a member of the Plymouth Argyle team that inflicted the heaviest defeat at Edgar Street in Hereford United's history, beating the Bulls 5-1. He was the Pilgrims' hero in a team that included Paul Mariner and Harry Burrows.

John was born in Hanworth, London, on 27 September 1953 and his talents as a schoolboy footballer soon attracted the football scouts in London. He was offered an apprenticeship with Queens Park Rangers and soon became an established member of their reserve side. He won an England Youth Cap and after one season with Rangers he made his first-team debut at the young age of nineteen, in a Second Division match against Luton Town at Kenilworth Road. John made another eight appearances that season, helping to maintain Rangers' bid for the title. They eventually finished the season in the runners-up spot, behind Burnley, and were duly promoted to the First Division. There were several big names at the club: Stan Bowles, Don Givens, Gerry Francis, Terry Venables and John Beck, many of whom went on to represent their country at international level, and John found it difficult to retain his first-team place. After playing in only 15 first-team games for Rangers, John was put on the transfer list as he sought regular first-team action. This resulted in him being signed by Plymouth Argyle in June 1974 for £25,000, and he made 132 appearances for the Pilgrims, scoring 6 goals. In his first season Argyle were runners-up in the Third Division, Hereford United finishing twelth.

In March 1978 John moved across the county to join Exeter City, where he spent five years. He played 216 games for Exeter, scoring 20 goals, before being released at the end of the 1982/83 season. John Newman, Hereford United's manager, recognised that John had great potential, and persuaded him to sign for the Bulls. During the next four years he proved him right by being a model professional and a very popular captain. After several seasons threatened with relegation and insolvency, it was a pleasure for Bulls fans to witness a change in fortunes as United finished midway in the table. The next season, 1984/85, was a memorable one as the Bulls staged a tremendous bid for promotion from the Fourth Division. Midway through the season Hereford United headed the table, John Delve leading the way with his excellent performances as club captain. He also played a huge part in the terrific win over his old club Plymouth Argyle in the second round of the FA Cup. This resulted in a fantastic third-round draw for United when the Gunners were drawn as their opposition. Unfortunately for John and the Hereford United fans, he sustained a nasty knee injury in the pre-Christmas home match against Aldershot and this resulted in him having surgery on his cartilage. John had to miss the two matches against Arsenal, and indeed missed the remainder of the season, and with another midfield player, Jimmy Harvey, on the injury list, the club narrowly missed out on promotion as they slipped to fifth place in the table. There are many supporters who felt that if John had not received that injury United would have maintained their position at the top of the League. His leadership qualities and experience were sorely missed; he was on top of his game before the injury.

The following season, 1985/86, John made his comeback and, although they did not perform quite so well in the League, they did get through to the area final of the Freight Rover Trophy against Bristol City, but lost 3-2 on aggregate. John made 38 League appearances and scored 6 goals for United in a season that saw them finish tenth in the League. After making 23 first-team appearances for the Bulls in the 1986/87 season and scoring 2 goals, John was given a free transfer by United. He moved into non-League football, playing for Gloucester City and then Minehead while working for the commercial department at Exeter City. Later in 1987 he rejoined Exeter City as a player, before eventually taking over the position of manager for a short while.

John will be best remembered by Bulls fans for his excellent performances in midfield, his inspiration as captain leading the team to many victories, and a great improvement in the fortunes of Hereford United.

Rob Elmes

Striker, 1999–2002

Rob Elmes was born in Cape Town in 1970 and did not play club football in England until he was twenty-three years of age, playing for Boldmere St Michaels. His nickname was 'Elmo' and he combined playing football with being a schoolteacher. When he was a schoolboy cricket was his game and he played for Dorset Under-16s as a batsman. As a schoolchild he was much smaller than his fellow pupils at Poole Grammar School and he never dreamt of being a footballer. However, by the time he studied at Keele University, gaining a 2.1 Honours degree in German and Classics he was a regular player in their football team as a central defender or midfielder, having grown rapidly in stature. He played so well that he was invited to go for a week's trial at Chester City, along with another student, but Rob Elmes declined, preferring to continue his studies. He first played club football while completing a year of his degree course in Hamburg, but only rarely playing on grass. Most of the games were played on a shale type surface, which Rob said 'certainly helped improve a player's technique'. On his return to England, after gaining his Certificate in Education, Rob took up a teaching post in Sutton Coldfield at Bishop Walsh RC School and started his English football career playing for Interlink Alliance club Boldmere St Michaels. He stayed with them until Christmas 1996 when he joined Bromsgrove Rovers. They played in the Conference League but Rob missed out on much of their unsuccessful attempt to avoid relegation through an eight-week long injury. He also had a spell at Macclesfield, who replaced Hereford United in the Football League, playing in front of crowds of 5,000 – a big change after playing for Boldmere – before joining Halesowen Town, who played in the Dr Martens Premier Division, where, in the 1998/99 season he switched to playing striker due to injury problems within the team. It worked out well, with them winning 13 out of the last 15 games, Steve Piearce scoring 20 goals and Rob 5. When Graham Turner offered Rob a part-time contract with Hereford United he jumped at the chance to join a club 'so steeped in soccer history'. He signed on a double free transfer with Steve Piearce in 1999. His partnership with Piearce was the reason both signed at the same time but in his first season with Hereford United he shared top marksman billing with Paul Fewings, both scoring 15 goals. He still combined his football with teaching PE and German. He had a very understanding headmaster who let Rob have time off when he needed it. He trained at Oldbury along with other members of the Hereford United squad, John Snape, Matt Gardiner and Kerry Giddings. He has been asked if he has ever sworn at the referee in German, but he replied, 'I've been tempted, but try to get the referee on my side with a bit of humour.' When he was sent off it was for foul and abusive language, in English. To make matters worse there were two of his pupils at the match!

Rob Elmes also took part in the FA Cup run that saw United play Leicester City. He missed their first-round tie against York City through injury, but was back in the side to play against Hartlepool in the next round. This match was screened live by Sky television and Rob scored the only goal of the game. He sees the matches against Leicester City that followed as the

Conference era

	Appearances	Goals
League	84 (27)	27
Other	8 (1)	3

Previous clubs: Boldmere St Michaels, Bromsgrove Rovers, Macclesfield Town, Halesowen Town highlight of his footballing career. It was an exciting time for Rob, with all the television stations wanting interviews. Many of his students had watched the game. He found the prospect of playing against defenders like Taggart, Elliott and Walsh a bit daunting, players he only knew from seeing them play on television, but over the two games there was not much between the two sides, Leicester City only managing to win 2-1 in extra time. The support at Filbert Street was tremendous, and Hereford United clung onto a 1-0 lead until twelve minutes from time when Leicester scored to take the game into extra time. Rob transferred to Moor Green where he continued to score goals, playing part-time.

Rob Elmes in action.

Elmes scores for Hereford against Burton Albion in the FA Trophy quarter-final, 10 March 2001. The match was televised live on Sky.

Steve Emery

Defender, 1972–1979, 1983–1985

Football League era

	Appearances	Goals
League	275(4)	12
Other	36 (2)	1

Previous clubs: Derby County

Steve Emery is a local lad who has the distinction of becoming Hereford United's first apprentice professional in June 1972 after they were elected to the Football League for the first time in their entire history. Steve was born in Ledbury in February 1956 and enjoyed playing in local football teams. He was also selected to play for the Herefordshire county youth team. He made his debut for Hereford United in a Border Counties League match against local rivals Worcester City in 1972 just after his sixteenth birthday, having previously played for Ledbury Town. His Football League debut was made at Newmarket Road against Cambridge United in February 1974 and he went on to make seven League appearances that season for United. The 1974/75 season saw Steve Emery really show what he was capable of; his full-back partnership with Tony Byrne was only broken three times all season. In a thrilling 6-3 victory over Blackburn Rovers in December 1974, the youthful qualities of Steve Emery linked up really well with the vintage passing and ball control of Terry Paine to take control of the game. Dixie McNeil scored the first goal for United following a neat pull-back by the talented Steve Emery. Steve was captain of the Hereford United team who took part in, and won, the Blauw Witt youth tournament in Amsterdam in the summer of 1975. He won a Third Division championship medal in the 1975/76 season when he only missed one game and scored two brilliant, unstoppable goals. The first came in a home match against Swindon Town after Terry Paine had stepped over a free-kick and Steve sent a great drive over the opponents' wall. The second was also scored at Edgar Street, this time in a 4-1 victory over Cardiff City, when he sent another wonderful free-kick into the top corner of the net. In the same season that the first team won the Third Division, Hereford United's youth side also won the Midland Intermediate Youth League. In the youth side were Kevin Sheedy, Chris Price and Steve Emery, who all went on to play in the Football League for the Bulls. Unfortunately, Steve missed the first fourteen games in the Second Division when the Bulls had a very mediocre few games after the excitement and hype of the previous season. They had won the first two home games against Hull City and Burnley but a run of dismal results, including the 6-1 defeat at home to Wolves and the 4-1 losses away to Fulham and at home to Notts County, found United near the wrong end of the table. Steve made 19 appearances for the Bulls that season and once he was again established in the team better results followed, but it was not enough to save the inevitable drop back to the Third Division. The 1977/78 season saw Steve Emery playing alongside John Layton, Steve Ritchie and Julian Marshall. It cannot be said that the back four let the team down, it was just a shame that the forward line could not put away a few more goals. There were 60 goals scored against United in the Football League that season, not catastrophic, but only 34 goals scored, which was relegation material. The following season saw Steve move into midfield, with a number of local players in the team, including Andy Feeley, Stewart Phillips and Paul Hunt. He only missed 3 League games all season and scored 5 League goals and 1 in the League Cup against Bristol Rovers. After seven years with Hereford United Steve moved to Derby County, who played in the First Division, for a fee of £100,000, a club record for United. The manager who snapped him up was none other than ex-Hereford United boss Colin Addison, who had also taken Hereford-born John Newman to the Baseball Ground as his number two. It was Colin who had originally signed Steve as an apprentice professional. Steve made his First Division debut two days after moving from Edgar Street and within a month of making the switch to the highest League of English football, Steve was made Man of the Match by a Sunday newspaper when Derby beat Bolton Wanderers 4-0 on Saturday 6 October 1979. He had two spells at Edgar Street and played 279 matches for United. His second spell at Edgar Street began at the start of the 1983/84 season in an exchange deal that saw Sean Lane move in the opposite direction. His final match for United was away against Aldershot, when they won 1-0 thanks to a goal from Larkin. After being released by Hereford United in 1985 he joined Wrexham before he retired from playing League football eighteen months later, returning to live in the Ledbury area.

From left to right: Steve Emery, Peter Isaac and manager John Newman in the Hereford United dressing room.

Brian Evans

Winger, 1973–1975

Football League era

	Appearances	Goals
League	44 (10)	9
Other	10	2

Previous clubs: Abergavenny Thursdays, Swansea Town

The signing of Brian Evans from Swansea prior to the start of the 1973/74 season proved to be a classic buy by manager Colin Addison. The Brynmawr-born player signed for Swansea Town from Welsh League club Abergavenny Thursdays in 1963. The Thursdays, as they were known locally, were originally formed by the town's shopkeepers and played their football on a Thursday afternoon, which was the town's early closing day. Evans enjoyed a number of successful seasons with Swansea and played for them in the Second, Third and Fourth Divisions. He made 356 appearances for the Swans, scoring 58 goals. During his time with the club they reached the FA Cup semi-final in 1964, losing to Preston North End. Often producing outstanding performances for his club, many football writers were puzzled by the fact Wales continually overlooked him.

Colin Addison brought Brian to Edgar Street at the start of the 1973/74 season; his first signing since United had won promotion to the Third Division. He marked his debut for Hereford by scoring a superb solo goal away at Grimsby Town after beating five players, in a wonderful 3-1 victory for the Bulls. By now he had at last been recognised by Wales and had gained 8 full caps to add to the 2 gained at Under-23 level. His first international was against Finland in a 3-0 win at the Vetch Field on 13 October 1971 and he also played against Czechoslovakia in Prague a fortnight later. At the time Wales were involved in a World Cup group with England and Poland, all attempting to qualify for the 1974 World Cup finals in Germany. Brian had played against England at Wembley in an inspired game that was drawn 1-1, which seriously dented England's chances but improved Wales'. Brian Evans became the first Hereford United player to gain a full international cap while playing for the club when he represented Wales against Poland at Chorzow on 26 September 1973, wearing the number seven shirt. Sadly, Wales lost 3-0, marking the end of their attempts to get to Germany and bringing down the curtain on Brian's international career, in front of a crowd of 120,000. Just prior to that match Brian had scored a fine individual goal at Edgar Street against Watford. He picked the ball up in his own half of the field and set off on a run down the wing, beating the inevitable, desperate challenges from the opposition. Cutting inside to the penalty area, he unleashed an unstoppable shot past goalkeeper Alan Rankin. In November 1973 Dudley Tyler was brought back to Hereford and he and Brian created dazzling displays out on each wing, some of the best football ever seen at Edgar Street. United had finished the 1973/74 campaign with only one defeat in their last ten matches. This good run took them clear of the bottom four and finally dispelled the fear of relegation, which at one time had looked a distinct possibility. The final league position was eighteenth with 43 points from 46 games, and Hereford were now firmly established in the Third Division. United gained the same number of points from away games as they had done in the previous promotion season, but at home they lost eight matches and only drew another five. Despite this the supporters continued to turn up and the average League attendance of over 8,000 was one of the highest in the division. At the end of the season Brian had scored a total of 9 goals for the club, making 30 full League appearances for United. He played his part in the FA Cup victory against West Ham United at Edgar Street, and gained a penalty for Hereford United after being tripped up in the penalty area by Keith Coleman. Tommy Naylor duly scored from the penalty spot, with Alan Jones scoring the winner. Brian ended an enjoyable first season for the club as joint top scorer with Jim Hinch, but was unhappy as he had lost his international place. Brian was keen to play in higher-graded football and was placed on the transfer list by Colin Addison, but withdrew his request the day after John Sillett was appointed manager in July 1974. The new season started brightly enough for Brian, winning the Man of the Match award in the first game against Aldershot. Several brilliant performances followed but in the match against Halifax Town at Edgar Street in October Brian was injured, and he failed to regain a regular place in the team. Brian played 44 League games in total for Hereford United, scoring 9 goals. He was released by Sillett on a free transfer, in March 1975, when the club could have asked for a fee, as a goodwill gesture for his excellent service, and he signed for Southern League side Bath City. Sadly Brian passed away just after his sixtieth birthday, but those who saw him play remember a truly gifted winger. There are many supporters who believe that he was possibly the most skilful player ever to play for United; his close ball control and body swerve were exceptional. In fact, many defenders described playing against him as torture; many goals were set up as a result of his accurate crossing ability.

John Galley

Striker/Defender, 1974–1977

Football League era

	Appearances	Goals
League	77 (3)	2
Other	5 (1)	

Previous clubs: Wolverhampton Wanderers, Rotherham United, Bristol City, Nottingham Forest

John Galley was a very versatile footballer of many talents who started off playing for Hereford United as a striker and then converted to a central defender. He will be best remembered for his leadership qualities as a target man and his towering displays at the heart of United's defence. John was born at Clowne in Derbyshire in May 1944 and after impressing at football in his teens he signed for Wolverhampton Wanderers at the age of seventeen. John only played in 5 first-team games at Molineux in three-and-a-half years, but scored twice, and then transferred to Rotherham United. It was here that his fortune changed for the better, and his bustling style of leadership gained him many appreciative fans. John scored 48 goals for the Millers in 112 games, helping them to become one of the top-scoring teams in the Second Division. In December 1967 Bristol City snapped him up for £25,000 and in that season he had the unique distinction of being top scorer not only for Bristol City but Rotherham United as well! John scored a hat-trick on his debut for the Robins in their 3-0 win over Huddersfield Town, and topped the goal-scoring charts for five seasons, scoring 22 goals in 1971/72. After 175 appearances for City John was transferred to Nottingham Forest for a fee of £30,000 in December 1972, striking 6 goals in 18 matches to make him their joint top scorer. The next thirteen matches were a big disappointment as John Galley had lost his goal-scoring knack, and this led to a two-month loan spell at Peterborough United in October 1974.

John Sillett was Hereford United's manager at this time and he became aware of John Galley's availability. He was able to capture his signature for a transfer fee of £4,000 in December 1974. He marked his debut at Edgar Street by scoring one of the goals in a 6-3 victory over Blackburn Rovers, the eventual champions. As his job was to replace Hereford United favourite Eric Redrobe, John Galley had a hard act to follow, especially in the eyes of the Bulls fans. However he quickly found his way into their hearts by netting 6 goals in 22 games, and instigating many of the chances put away by his fellow striker Dixie McNeil. He was converted into a central defender during the summer with the arrival of Steve Davey at Edgar Street and was an outstanding

Galley in action.

success. John had great aerial ability and his organisational skills at the back helped United to win the Third Division championship with a consistent run of 35 League matches at the centre of the Bulls' defence. Indeed, during November 1975, when John had to undergo an operation on his cartilage and had to miss nine matches for United, his presence was sorely missed. After losses to Brighton, Walsall and Shrewsbury, many supporters felt that the chance of winning the championship trophy had gone. His return to the team towards the end of January marked a change in fortune for the Bulls. A 4-1 away win at Layer Road, home of Colchester United, was the start of a run of matches that saw the Bulls lose only 4 matches out of 24. They won the championship title by six points, having scored 41 goals during the season, John Galley claiming 2. His first goal was against Southend United and scored at Edgar Street in the final minute of the game to give United maximum points, Dixie having scored the first. His second was at home to Halifax when Galley switched from defender to attacker to drive in a ten-yard equaliser, but Halifax stole the points with a ninetieth-minute winner. The following season was a bit of a disaster for United; they had the regrettable distinction of being the first team to have won the Third Division championship one year and the following year finish bottom of the Second Division and thus be relegated. There were highlights though: United reached the final of the Welsh FA Cup and they scored five goals away from home, at Oldham, for the first time in a Football League match. The season was a difficult one, with many injuries to key players, which saw John Galley playing in both defence and attack. This was his last season in the Football League. He made 20 appearances for United and scored another 2 goals against Leyton Orient and Blackpool, taking his tally of League goals to over 150. John stayed in football, playing for Telford United and Atherstone Town, before progressing to be youth development officer at Nottingham Forest. He will be fondly remembered by many United fans for his versatility and leadership qualities, his great aerial presence, which led to many goals for his teammates, most notably Dixie McNeil, and his great displays at the heart of United's defence in the 1975/76 championship-winning team.

Galley celebrates while Steve Davey and Dixie McNeil run to congratulate the scorer.

Ricky George

Winger, 1971–1972

Prior to 1972/73

Appearances	Goals
45	8

Previous clubs: Tottenham Hotspur, Watford, Bournemouth, Oxford United, Barnet

Ricky George described the team of 1971/72 as a great team – a truly great team. He was desperate to get on the pitch during the home game against Newcastle United in the FA Cup after being named as substitute for the match, as he had been for most of that season. He eventually came on to replace the unlucky Roger Griffiths, who broke his leg in a collision with Fred Potter, United's goalkeeper, and helped set up the first goal for Hereford United, which was scored by Ronnie Radford. Coming onto the pitch in the eighty-first minute, Ricky felt that he only had nine minutes to do something, anything. He chased every ball, determined not to waste the opportunity. He won the ball on eighty-seven minutes, chasing back on the left flank, and slipped the ball inside for Ken Mallender to knock first time into midfield. Ron Radford challenged for the ball and, after a one-two with Brian Owen, scored. Radford later returned the compliment in the 103rd minute, the game having gone to extra time. Ron Radford, thirty yards from goal, pushed the ball six yards to Dudley Tyler, who cut inside to gain some space. Ricky was waiting on the edge of the penalty area and Dudley drove the ball straight at him with his left foot. Ricky George managed to control the ball with his second touch, turning at the same time, and struck the ball right-footed towards goal, across the outstretched leg of the Newcastle captain Bobby Moncur, into the back of the net, with their goalkeeper McFaul nowhere near it. 'The goal was somewhere near, so I just tried my luck' was one of the numerous quotes from Ricky George. He admits to still feeling emotional about the goal some thirty years on; he knew he had done something very, very special, after all the previous failures and disappointments. The Sunday papers were full of praise for Hereford United and in particular for the two goalscorers, Ricky George and Ronnie Radford. The Sunday Mirror said, 'carpenter Ron Radford and sales rep Ricky George, carved with pride the name of Hereford into the FA Cup history book. They will be remembered as the men who gave Hereford the record of being the first non-League club to beat a First Division team in the cup for twenty-two years.' The Sunday Telegraph wrote, 'Hereford kept waiting like an impatient bride for their three-times-postponed third-round tie, swept Newcastle out of the FA Cup, they then invited West Ham to a delayed fourth-round reception

Ricky George

Winger, 1971–1972

West Ham players mark Ricky George at Edgar Street.

in the same parish. Best man at yesterday's affair was substitute Ricky George'. Although scoring the goal was so important to Ricky, he admits to feeling that the Giant-killers were very lucky people. He quoted Bill Shankly who once said that he had told his players time and time again that they were playing for the fans, for the people of Liverpool. A football club only exists to serve the community.

He was born in Barnet in June 1946 and became a Barnet supporter at the early age of seven, his brother having joined the club as a member of the playing staff. Ricky played for Wood Green & District Under-15s team and represented Hertfordshire Schools against Middlesex, Surrey and Suffolk. The match against Suffolk was played on Ipswich Town's ground and Hertfordshire won 6-2, with Ricky George scoring twice. He attended the White Hart Lane training pitches twice a week to train with other schoolboys and, when Ricky left school, he became an apprentice at Tottenham Hotspur in October 1963. However, he was unable to get in their first team, which included such names as Jimmy Greaves, Danny Blanchflower and Dave Mackay. It was at this time that he gained an interest in horse racing, which was to give him another extra-special event in his life. Ricky moved to Watford in August 1964 and made his League debut for the Vicarage Road club at Port Vale when he was eighteen. Their full-back was Ken Nicholas and he lived in Barnet, so Ricky George became his chauffeur, taking him to and from Watford. Ricky then transferred to Bournemouth and, after spending a season there, moved to Oxford United in July 1966. After 6 appearances for Oxford, Ricky moved to Hastings, where he was paid £18 per week. He scored a hat-trick in his first match in a 5-1 win over Queens Park Rangers reserves and it was not long before he was snapped up by Barnet. Here he

Ricky George

Winger, 1971–1972

scored nearly 50 goals in just under three seasons before being signed up by John Charles to join Hereford United for a £600 fee in March 1971 to link up with Billy Meadows, with whom he had played at Barnet. Billy had called Ricky George three times the previous November telling him that he was wanted at Edgar Street, but it took months to complete the transfer as Ricky sustained a bad ankle injury. Once he got to the Bulls' ground he felt that it was an honour to play alongside the footballing legend John Charles. Ricky George was paid the vast sum of £25 per week during the football season and £15 per week during the close season. Ricky joined as a part-time player, training at Underhill Road and working part-time for Adidas, dealing with international players of both Scotland and England. Just two seasons after being beaten by Hereford United, Newcastle United reached the final of the FA Cup where their opponents were Liverpool. In his capacity as Adidas Soccer Public Relations person it was Ricky's job to meet up with the Newcastle squad at their hotel on the eve of the match. As he strode into the lobby, the late Joe Harvey, Newcastle's manager, was standing with his assistant, the future Tottenham Hotspur boss Keith Burkenshaw. The look on their faces would have been worth filming, until they realised Ricky was there in an official capacity. It was almost the same team that had been beaten by Hereford, which just goes to proves how good an achievement that win was.

Ricky made 45 appearances for Hereford United, very often as a substitute, mainly in the Southern League. He was quoted as saying that the 1971/72 Hereford United team was the best non-League team ever put together. Five days after the victory over Newcastle United Ricky George played the full ninety minutes against West Ham in front of an enthusiastic 14,819 crowd. He lined up opposite Harry Redknapp on West Ham's right wing; they are the same age and had played against each other in Spurs *v.* West Ham youth matches. All of a sudden, the unknown players from the backwater of Hereford were famous. All the national papers were after photographs of the players. The *Evening Standard* produced a souvenir edition that paired Ricky George with Bobby Moore on the front page, something to be cherished for years. Ricky George returned to Underhill Road, first as a player, playing under manager Billy Meadows and then as a director and vice-chairman of Barnet Football Club, but experienced mixed fortunes with the club, with boardroom squabbles and the club in fear of going into liquidation. Ricky then became a Tottenham Hotspur fan, along with his family.

In 1992 Ricky was offered a sixth share in the racehorse Earth Summit, the BBC television commentator John Motson having turned down the same offer. The horse cost £5,800 in total and won the Grand National in 1998, beating previous winners Rough Quest and Suny Bay by eleven lengths. Earth Summit was proven over long distances, a brilliant jumper, a mudlark happy in the most extreme conditions, game and genuine. Unfortunately he sustained a small injury in training and the decision was taken to retire him in January 2000.

John Motson and Ricky George had remained friends since the early giant-killing days and John once described Ricky as unreliable but one of the most generously spirited people he has ever met. He is a man of many talents, including regular radio interviews and writing a column for the *Daily Telegraph*.

Bobby Gould

Striker, 1978–1979

Football League era

	Appearances	Goals
League	42 (3)	13
Other	2 (1)	0

Previous clubs: Coventry City, Arsenal, Wolverhampton Wanderers, West Bromwich Albion, West Ham United, Bristol City, Bristol Rovers

Bobby Gould first came to the attention of Hereford United fans in October 1976 – when playing for the opposition! Hereford United were beaten 6-1 by Wolverhampton Wanderers in a Second Division match at Edgar Street that most Bulls fans would rather forget – it was United's heaviest defeat at home. Bobby scored Wolves' third and fifth goals and missed two easy chances, and at the end of the season Wolves went on to lift the Second Division championship, whereas United ended up being relegated.

Robert Gould was born in Coventry in June 1946 and joined Coventry City as an apprentice before signing for the club as a full professional. With Bobby's help, Coventry won promotion to the First Division in the 1966/67 season, Bobby scoring 24 goals to make him the Second Division's top scorer. He scored a total of 40 goals in 81 games for the Sky Blues and in 1968 he was transferred to Arsenal for a 'substantial fee'. He played for the Gunners in the 1969 Football League Cup final, when they lost, very surprisingly, to Swindon Town, before being transferred to Wolverhampton Wanderers for £55,000 at the end of the 1969/70 season. Wolves were playing in the First Division and at the end of Bobby Gould's first season they finished fourth in the League. Bobby scored 17 goals and finished top scorer, including a hat-trick against Manchester United. He also managed five goals in the Texaco Cup, a competition that Wolves won by beating Hearts 3-2 on aggregate in the final. In 1971 Bobby moved to West Bromwich Albion for £60,000 and the following year he moved to Bristol City as a replacement for John Galley for a £70,000 fee (a club record for City). West Ham were the next team to sign Bobby Gould before he rejoined Wolverhampton Wanderers in 1975. In 1977 Bristol Rovers signed Bobby as player-coach and he scored a hat-trick on his debut as Blackburn Rovers were beaten 4-1.

In September 1978 Mike Bailey, a former Wolves player and skipper, was manager of Hereford United and he signed Bobby Gould as assistant manager for a £10,000 fee. Apparently Mike and Bobby had a gentlemen's agreement that whoever had a job first in management would take the other on as their assistant. Mike Bailey had also starred in the 6-1 rout of United by Wolves and they now combined again for

Gould shoots for goal.

an identical scoreline, but this time in United's favour. Crewe were the opposition at Edgar Street and Bobby scored the first and fourth goals and set up the second. Many fans had chosen to stay away from the ground after United's poor start to the season – what a match to miss! It was later revealed that Bobby had played in some ancient boots he had patched up especially for the game. They were his 'lucky boots', in which he had scored a hat-trick on his debut for Bristol Rovers. The victory against Crewe was followed up by a 2-0 win away at Rochdale, when Bobby found the back of the net again. This was United's first away win in 32 matches! At the end of the season Bobby had scored 13 goals, making him United's top scorer, and he had taken his career total to 160 goals. Bobby Gould made a further five appearances for Hereford United in the 1979/80 season before being persuaded by Geoff Hurst to move to Chelsea as assistant manager. With his help they finished fourth in the Second Division, missing out on promotion to Birmingham City on goal average. Bobby later assisted at Aldershot and Wimbledon before managing Bristol Rovers (twice) and Coventry City. While at Coventry in 1983/84 Bobby Gould turned out for them in a Central League game when they were short of players, and managed to score a goal. He pulled on a Hereford United shirt again later that season when the Bulls were also short of players, in a Combination game, but on this occasion United lost 3-0. When Wimbledon lost their manager Dave Bassett to Watford the South London club appointed Bobby Gould as his replacement. He and Don Howe combined to pull off one of the most remarkable FA Cup final upsets of all time, when Wimbledon beat Liverpool 1-0 in 1988 to win the trophy. Bobby later had managerial spells with West Bromwich Albion and Coventry City before becoming a television pundit for Sky Television for eighteen months. This was followed, in 1995, by Bobby being appointed the Welsh international team manager. Bobby will best be remembered for his bubbly character and supreme confidence, which seemed to inspire his teammates. He loved his football and was impressed by the support the club got from the people in the city. He once said 'You've got to make the greatest use of any talent that you've got, that's all I've ever tried to do.'

Harry Gregory

Midfield, 1972–1974

Football League era

	Appearances	Goals
League	71 (2)	5
Other	2	0

Previous clubs: Leyton Orient, Charlton Athletic, Aston Villa

Harry Gregory will be remembered by the Hereford United fans for all the right reasons – and also all the wrong reasons. His superb ball control, passing and determination were a credit to him, but his other antics on the pitch and arguing got him into a lot of strife with officials on the pitch and the football club.

Gordon Gregory was born at Buckhurst Hill, London on 24 October 1943, but he was always known as 'Harry'. His skills on the football field were spotted at an early age and Harry joined the Leyton Orient ground staff straight from school. While a junior at Brisbane Road Harry won both England Schoolboy and England Youth international honours. On his eighteenth birthday he was immediately signed on as a professional but had to wait until 1962 before making his League debut. During the next three seasons Harry made 79 League appearances, scoring 11 goals, before being transferred to Charlton Athletic in August 1966. In his four seasons at The Valley he made another 149 League appearances and scored 24 goals after becoming a regular in the heart of their midfield. Aston Villa clinched his signature in October 1970 for a fee of £7,000 after being relegated to the Third Division. Harry put in some tremendous performances to lead Villa back to the Second Division but the following season saw Harry plagued by injury and he was unable to reclaim his place. In August 1972 he was signed by Colin Addison, along with another Villa player, David Rudge, for a combined fee of £11,000. They provided an excellent balance to the midfield and they became firm favourites with the United fans during the Bulls' first season in the Football League. There was no doubt that Harry had great ability and flair, but he was also very unpredictable and had a volatile nature, which endeared him to many fans but frequently got him into trouble with the hierarchy at the club. At the end of his first season at Edgar Street, when he had made 39 appearances for the Bulls, scoring 3 goals, Harry had been fined over £100 through bookings and suspensions. 'It has been my own fault,' Harry admitted, 'It's not as if I'm getting booked for serious things. Just silly trivial things like arguing. I've got no-one to blame but myself.' The qualities that got Harry into trouble also helped him to gain the captain's armband. 'I jumped at the chance of being captain, I shout a lot anyway. Even in training I tend to tell players what to do, it just comes naturally. Being so much involved in the game has an effect on my disciplinary record though. I think I perhaps become so involved in the game that when I'm pulled up for something I just flare up. Or when things aren't going right for us I become too aggressive in trying to remedy it.' Harry likened life at Edgar Street to that at Villa Park, saying that Hereford is a mini-Villa. After being substituted in the second half of a match at home to Wrexham in October 1973 by manager Colin Addison he threw off his shirt in disgust, and this was reported in the headlines of the *Daily Telegraph*! An apology from Harry was printed in the Bulls' programme the following home game, when he explained that he meant no disrespect to club supporters or player-manager Colin Addison. This apology earned him brownie points with the fans and the sports writer at the *Telegraph*, who wrote 'It is a point that should be digested by certain players in the higher echelons of the League.' Colin Addison commented, 'It takes character to say you are sorry.' In the next match for United Harry gave a superb performance away at Port Vale, providing the crosses for two out of three goals scored by the Bulls. After making 21 appearances in that season, scoring 2 goals, Harry was told that he would need an operation on an Achilles tendon injury just four days before the start of the next season, an injury that was to keep him out of the game for at least three months. John Sillett described this as 'a tragic blow', saying, 'Any team is bound to miss a player of his ability.' After recovering from injury, but failing to get back into the starting line-up, Harry demanded to be put on the transfer list. Sillett agreed to his request but said at the time that he thought Harry was acting hastily. After making 11 appearances for United Harry left at the end of the season, joining Southern League team Chelmsford.

A spell in prison underlined the darker side of Harry's nature but he will best be remembered for his skills on the pitch, his superb crossing of the ball, his scissor-kicks and back heels and his abrasive style of play and antics on the pitch. His spirit and determination helped United to gain promotion from the Fourth Division at their first attempt.

Gregory celebrates a goal.

Roger Griffiths

Defender, 1963–1968, 1970–1973

Prior to 1972/73

	Appearances	Goals
	241	0

Football League era

	Appearances	Goals
League	7 (2)	0
Other	0	0

Previous clubs: Worcester City

Roger Griffiths is a local lad, who has been Player of the Year for both Hereford United and local rivals Worcester City. He was born in Hereford in February 1945 and was one of the few players who played for Hereford United in both the Southern League and the Football League. He was the only local player in the famous 'Giant-killing' team of the 1970s. Roger grew up supporting Hereford United. As a boy he used to watch them both at home and away with his dad.

Roger signed for the Bulls in 1963 as an amateur before turning professional the following year, after having been on the books of Bristol City. He made his first-team debut in 1964. Following relegation the previous season, Hereford United had their best ever start to the season in 1964. They drew away against Deal Town on the opening Saturday and followed this up with winning nine league matches in a row. Local interest started to grow in the club again and when Wimbledon visited Edgar Street in their first season in the Southern League, the attendance was 5,123. Wimbledon spoilt the party, however, by beating United 2-1, even though Hereford had taken the lead. United went on to clinch promotion with six matches still to play and eventually won the First Division title by eleven points from second-placed Wimbledon, who they beat 2-1 in the return match at Plough Lane. The average attendance for league matches at Edgar Street was up 1,000 on the previous season. There were several big victories including a 7-0 victory against Trowbridge Town, a team which included Colin Tavener, who eventually joined United in 1972. The 1965/66 season was another good one for United: they finished third back in the Premier Division and reached the third round of the FA Cup for only the second time in their history. After away victories at Cheltenham and Leytonstone, United were rewarded with a home tie against Millwall and a crowd of 11,940 shared their 1-0 victory.

In the Southern League match between Hereford United and Bedford Town at the start of the 1966/67 season Roger made history for United. This opening match of the season saw the introduction of substitutes for the first time and, when Roger Griffiths replaced Peter McCall for the second half in a 5-1 win for

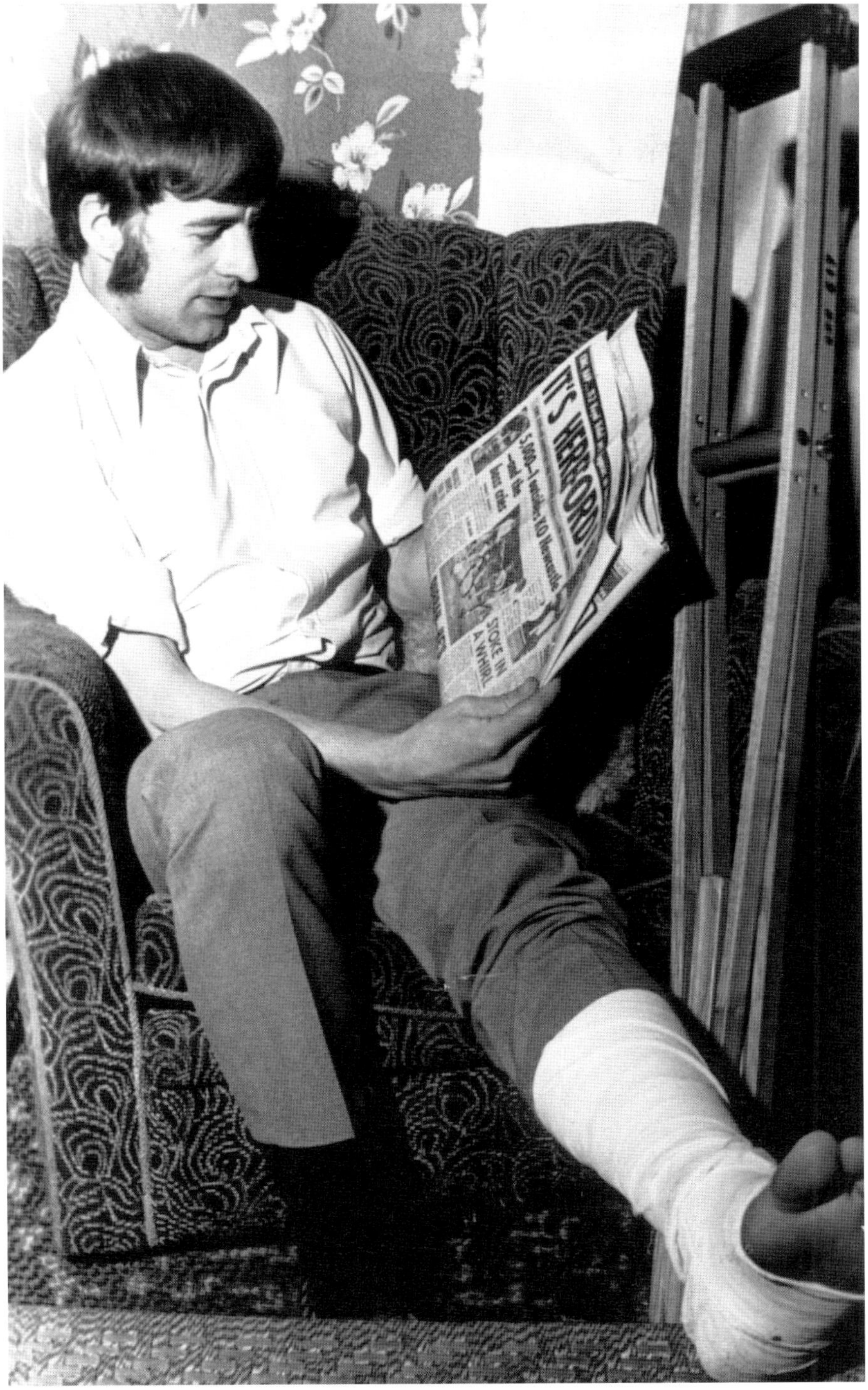

Injured hero Roger Griffiths reads all about the Newcastle match in a Sunday newspaper.

United, he became the club's first ever substitute. He played in 141 games for United and was Player of the Year at the end of the 1967/68 season, but moved to Worcester City following a wages dispute.

Roger returned to Edgar Street in 1970 to feature prominently for United in the next three years. He typified the never-say-die attitude of the team at that time by playing for seventy-six minutes against Newcastle United at Edgar Street with a broken leg. He was injured within five minutes of kick-off in a collision with Hereford United's goalkeeper Fred Potter when challenged by Malcolm Macdonald, and carried on despite the pain. He felt something crack and was in pain whenever he tackled the opposition but no-one guessed he was in trouble, least of all the Newcastle players. However, once Newcastle scored Roger decided it was time for him to go off as he was not able to overlap as much as usual. An X-ray after the match had finished revealed that he had broken his fibula. Roger was included in the West Ham programme team list for United as they said he did not deserve to be the 'Forgotten Man'.

Roger made 250 appearances for Hereford United, usually as a full-back or defensive wing half. Nine appearances for the Bulls were in the Football League, two of which were as a substitute. He went on to play for Gloucester City in the Southern League and for Kington Town (as player-manager) and Llandrindod Wells in the Mid Wales League. Roger Griffiths continues to live locally, working for Sun Valley in the maintenance department. Every year when the FA Cup comes round the tremendous memories come flooding back. Roger believes that United could have lifted the FA Cup if they had beaten West Ham. The confidence in the Bulls camp was sky high after their victory over Newcastle. 'It was one of the most exciting times of my life and the belief in the team was unbelievable.' Sadly, after his injury, he missed both of the matches against the Hammers and he did not get the chance to play against the legendary World Cup hero Bobby Moore. However, Roger was delighted to be involved in a radio interview with the late England captain, shortly before the first match against West Ham at Edgar Street. Unfortunately he never got to hear it because it went out live on national radio!

Jimmy Harvey

Midfield, 1980–1987

Football League era

	Appearances	Goals
League	276 (2)	39
Other	31 (1)	7

Previous clubs: Glenavon, Arsenal

Jimmy Harvey brought skill, great ball control and a touch of class to Hereford United's midfield when he joined in 1980. James Harvey was born in Lurgan, County Armagh, in Northern Ireland on 2 May 1958. He played for Glenavon in the Irish League before Arsenal brought him to England in August 1977 in a £30,000 deal. He was a regular in the Gunners' reserves and featured strongly in the two Football Combination matches against the Bulls' reserve side in 1978. Jimmy Harvey represented Northern Ireland at Youth and Under-21 levels and was selected three times for the full international squad. However, a first-team place was beckoning and Jimmy Harvey made his Football League debut for Arsenal in the last match of the 1977/78 season, away to Derby County, playing alongside Graham Rix and Liam Brady. He made his Highbury debut at the start of the following season against Leeds United in the First Division, Liam Brady scoring both goals in a 2-2 draw. A crowd of over 42,000 saw him line up alongside Pat Jennings, David O'Leary, Malcolm Macdonald and Frank Stapleton. Jimmy Harvey only played in three First Division games and was approached by Hereford United during the 1979/80 season to consider coming to Edgar Street. He came on loan, making 11 appearances in a two-month spell, before signing in the summer, and eventually stayed for seven seasons when he became a firm favourite with the Edgar Street faithful. In his first full season with Hereford United, Jimmy Harvey suffered various knocks and injuries and only made 29 appearances for the club, but the following season he firmly established himself in the team, and became an automatic choice for manager Frank Lord. He made 42 League appearances and scored 5 League goals. He was a stylish midfield player with great passing ability and good ball control, who was particularly dangerous at set pieces. He became club captain and was recognised by all who played in the Fourth Division as an exceptional player. He was selected by the other players as a member of the PFA Fourth Division XI for four consecutive seasons 1983 to 1987. He was only the second player to gain a place in the team four years running since the awards were instituted in 1973, following in the footsteps of Bulls defender Chris Price. One of Jimmy's assets was knowing the qualities of other players and how best to utilise them. In particular he built up a great understanding with Chris Price on the right wing. He used to pass the ball out for Chris, with his amazing pace, to run on to and take into the box, which resulted in numerous penalty claims as Chris was brought down in and around the box. The Bulls' spot-kick taker was none other than Jimmy Harvey. He was called up to train with the Northern Ireland international squad, but to the surprise of many never received a full cap.

He played in United's famous victory in the Welsh Cup final against Swansea in May 1981 and also the infamous FA Cup games against Arsenal. Jimmy threw the ball into Chris Price's path to enable him to score United's goal past John Lukic in the 1-1 draw in the FA Cup third round on 5 January 1985. Jimmy was inspirational in this match. Unfortunately he sustained an injury playing against Mansfield Town away from home and was out for several weeks, regretably at the same time as John Delve. This combined loss in midfield meant that Hereford United would struggle for the remainder of the season. What started off as a very promising season with promotion well within their grasp halfway through, turning out to be a big disappointment with United missing out on promotion by just one place, although seven points adrift of fourth-placed Bury. Harvey made a total of 276 appearances for United, scoring 38 goals before being transferred by United's manager John Newman to Bristol City for a meagre (some thought) £20,000 fee. His last appearance for Hereford United was at home against Hartlepool United. He was injured in the seventeenth minute and had to be substituted by Butler. He only made three appearances for Bristol before being loaned to Wrexham and then being transferred to Tranmere Rovers. Harvey immediately led his new club to promotion from the old Fourth Division and the old Third Division in successive seasons. He made over 180 appearances for Rovers before joining the coaching staff at Tranmere Rovers and then Crewe Alexandra. He is currently manager of Morecambe who, like Hereford United, are playing in the Conference.

Tommy Hughes

Goalkeeper, 1973–1981

Football League era

	Appearances	Clean sheets
League	240	64
Other	31	12

Previous clubs: Clydebank, Chelsea, Aston Villa

Tommy Hughes was arguably the finest goalkeeper ever to play for Hereford United and is certainly a firm favourite with many of the older generation of Hereford fans. Tommy first appeared at Edgar Street in March 1973 as an Aston Villa player, the reason being the official opening of the Len Weston stand. This stand holds 1,200 spectators and had cost £31,000. Work was completed in December 1972 to give complete covered accommodation on all four sides of the Edgar Street ground. Aston Villa were invited to visit Edgar Street to mark the official opening of the stand. To many Hereford fans present that night, Tommy Hughes was merely the opposition goalkeeper. The game ended in a 2-2 draw with Villa winning on penalties. After the match, as Tommy left with his Villa teammates, he probably never expected to be returning to Edgar Street in the near future.

Newly promoted Hereford United played their first match in the Third Division on Saturday 25 August 1973 away at Grimsby Town. The 3-1 result in Hereford's favour was marred by the injury to goalkeeper Fred Potter, who broke his wrist. This sadly was the last competitive match Fred played for the club. A new 'keeper had to be found as David Icke had also had to retire with medical problems. Colin Addison, the manager, needed to sign a goalkeeper quickly and he duly signed Tommy Hughes from Aston Villa for a then-record £12,000 fee. On Wednesday 29 August 1973 Hughes made his debut for Hereford United in an away League Cup fixture against Cardiff City. Perhaps not the greatest of games for Tommy in a Hereford shirt, the match ended in a 2-0 defeat. Hereford's first home match in the Third Division occurred on Saturday 1 September 1973, when Tommy Hughes was introduced to the home fans, which resulted in a 1-0 win for United, Harry Gregory scoring the only goal of the match in the sixty-eighth minute.

His signing proved to be a remarkable purchase of a player who was loyal to the club for the rest of his playing days. His superb performances in goal that season led to his Player of the Year award at the end; he had missed only two of the club's remaining fifty-three matches. It was the start of an affectionate relationship between Tommy and the club's supporters and he won the award again in 1979 to join Billy Tucker as the only other player to receive the trophy on two occasions.

Tommy Hughes

Goalkeeper, 1973–1981

Tommy Hughes makes another fine save.

Tommy made 240 Football League appearances for Hereford United and the total might have been considerably more if he had not broken his leg in training at the start of the 1980/81 season. Fighting his way back to full fitness, he resumed as the club's first-team goalkeeper again at the start of what was to be his last season, 1981/82, playing in United's first seventeen League and cup games until an arthritic elbow forced him to seek specialist treatment. After playing three Combination games further problems occurred, which forced him to retire from playing at the end of the 1981/82 season. He later served the club as acting commercial manager and for a time as manager of the team.

During his time playing for the club Tommy had some memorable battles with opposing strikers. Perhaps there are some that can remember the way he stood up to Bobby Gould, who always tried to intimidate Tommy when he was the visiting striker. One can only speculate as to what was said when they later became teammates at Hereford United.

During nine seasons at Edgar Street, Tommy Hughes made 355 appearances for Hereford United in the Second, Third and Fourth Divisions, FA Cup, Football League Cup, Welsh Cup, Herefordshire Senior Cup, Football Combination, Midland Intermediate League and Northern Floodlight League.

Born in Oalmuir, Scotland, Tommy Hughes' goalkeeping career apparantly began with some reluctance. He was told to step into the breach when the regular goalkeeper at St Stephen's School failed to appear for a Saturday morning match. He was only ten years old and had to do what he was told. Luckily the master in charge made a wise decision because Tommy saved a penalty and in the process took the first step towards a professional career that brought him Scottish Under-23 international honours, gaining 2 caps. Although he was given trials, no professional football club signed him. When he left school he became an apprentice electrician and it was while he was playing with Scottish junior club Clydebank Athletic that a string of fine performances started to attract outside interest. It had always been his schoolboy dream to play for Celtic and it looked as though his big chance had arrived when he was invited to sign amateur forms for the Glasgow club, who were then the reigning Scottish League champions. In later years Tommy recalled, 'I was due to sign for Celtic on the Thursday but on the Tuesday night there was a knock on the door at home and the local scout for Chelsea said that Tommy Docherty wanted me to join the club. Hughes was seventeen when he arrived at Stamford Bridge in 1965 as understudy to England international Peter Bonetti, and the following year he made his First Division debut. But during his six seasons with the London club he played mainly in the Football Combination.

In March 1969 he was selected to play for the Scottish Under-23 team against England at Roker Park, Sunderland, but it is a game he would rather forget. England romped to a 3-1 lead and the game was abandoned in the sixtieth minute due to snow. He did return to his native Glasgow that December to play against France at Hampden Park. Scotland won 4-0 and Tommy kept a clean sheet. Although happy at Stamford Bridge, Tommy was ambitious for regular first-team football. After breaking his leg on a pre-season tour in Holland in 1970 he was out of action for several months and the following year he was transferred to Aston Villa for a £12,500 fee. He played for Villa in their first sixteen League matches of the 1971/72 season but when he was injured in the November it left the club with a goalkeeping problem, whereupon they went to West Bromwich Albion and signed the club's first-choice goalkeeper Jimmy Cumbes for a £35,000 fee. Cumbes played in the remaining matches to help Villa clinch the Third Division championship.

Tommy Hughes' reaction when being told that Hereford United wanted to sign him was 'Where is Hereford?' Now considered a Herefordian by all, Tommy has continued to live and work in the city and is fondly remembered by many United fans.

Hughes punches clear while defender Alan Jones ducks.

Peter Isaac

Goalkeeper, 1960–1968, 1970–1971

Prior to 1972//73

	Appearances	Clean sheets
	258	94

Previous clubs: Stoke City, Barry Town, Northampton Town

William Henry Isaac was born in Pontypridd in South Wales in May 1935 and eventually spent over thirty years at Edgar Street, where he was known by all as 'Peter', serving under thirteen different managers. As a schoolboy he was a rugby player and a boxer, doing well at both sports, but eventually Peter decided on a career in football after being chosen to play for Wales against England in a youth international at Fratton Park, the home of Portsmouth. In March 1953 Peter joined Stoke City, but shortly afterwards was called up for his national service with the Royal Horse Guards. During his time in the Army he won representative honours with the Northern Command and on his discharge he rejoined Stoke City. Eventually he joined the Welsh football team Barry Town after failing to make an appearance for Stoke. In July 1958 Peter signed for Northampton Town where he played in 8 Football League games for the Cobblers in the 1958/59 season. He joined Hereford United in 1960 after gentle persuasion from the Bulls' manager at that time, Joe Wade. He made a total of 353 appearances in goal for United, including 258 Southern League games. Although he chose football, Peter continued his interest in rugby and boxing, and rated Hereford Rugby Club as one of his favourite 'other teams'. Two very important football matches that Peter Isaacs took part in were in the FA Cup games against Millwall, which United won 1-0, and away to Bristol City, which resulted in a 1-1 draw. Peter also played in both legs of the Welsh Cup final against Cardiff City in May 1968. The away leg at Ninian Park was the last appearance for Peter Isaacs in Hereford United team colours for the time being as he then moved to St George's Lane, the home of the Bulls' local rivals Worcester City. He spent twelve months as the first-choice goalkeeper for Worcester before moving across the county to join Kidderminster Harriers. In July 1970 Peter returned to Edgar Street to help out John Charles, United's player-manager, and when United were elected to the Football League two years later he became a full-time member of the non-playing staff. During his thirty-plus seasons at Edgar Street he was a player, coach, physiotherapist, trainer and caretaker-manager and a backroom boy. The managers he served under, besides 'Big John' and Joe Wade, were Ray Daniel, Bob Dennison, Colin Addison, John Sillett, Tony Ford, Mike Bailey, Frank Lord,

Tommy Hughes, John Newman, Ian Bowyer and Greg Downs. He saw the highs and lows of football at Edgar Street, the bliss of promotion, the pain of relegation, and the agony of re-election. Peter was very popular at Edgar Street with the players and fans alike. He always found the time to enjoy banter with supporters, with a smile for the young and the not so young. Everyone respected the outstanding service that Peter gave to their football club. At away games he always spoke to the Hereford United supporters who had travelled to see their favourite team play. Peter was awarded for his long service to the Bulls when he was awarded a benefit match against Manchester United in 1992. The famous First Division team had promised to bring their first-team squad to Edgar Street but many Hereford United supporters were extremely disappointed when they changed their minds and only sent their reserve team to the home of the Bulls. Alex Ferguson took his first team to Scandinavia for a (more financially rewarding) tour, much to the dismay of many. Peter Hill, who was chairman of Hereford United at the time of his benefit match, paid tribute to Peter as follows: 'Peter Isaac has a unique record of service, to Hereford United in particular and football in general, and there are few people in the country from the Premier League to Sunday soccer who could equal the years of dedication he has given to the game over three decades. When he first joined the club in 1960 I was already a diehard supporter and used to watch the club's Southern League games from the terraces of Edgar Street, and I can remember the rivalry Peter had with Gerry Sewell to establish himself as United's first-choice goalkeeper. As club chairman I cannot speak too highly of what Peter did over the years to enhance the reputation of Hereford United. He was willing to turn his hand to anything to help the club and always displayed loyalty, determination, dedication and sportsmanship. He was a wonderful ambassador and well deserved the tribute of the benefit match against Manchester United that marked thirty years of outstanding service.'

Goalkeeper Peter Isaac in action for Hereford United.

Tony James

Defender, 1998–

Conference era

	Appearances	Goals
League	215 (7)	16
Other	21 (1)	3

Previous clubs: Cardiff City, West Bromwich Albion, Tranmere Rovers

Tony James was born in Cwmbran in 1978 and started playing in football matches at the age of six for local clubs. He very often played in teams of boys two years older than himself before he joined Cwmbran Celtic at the age of fourteen. In local football Cwmbran Celtic were the team to be in and with them Tony won nearly every local competition possible. He also played rugby for his school, Croesyceiliog, as this was the only way the boys could get into the football team! However, Tony James did not relish playing rugby; football was his favourite sport. In rugby he usually played at outside half, hoping that one of the other backs would be tackled before the ball reached him! In his early teens he signed schoolboy forms for Cardiff City but they did not further their interest, so when Tony was about to leave school he considered doing a physical education course. However, a friend suggested that Tony James be invited to make up a West Bromwich Albion team that were due to play an England Under-16s team at Lilleshall but who were a man short. Tony was then asked to play in a couple more matches and was then taken on by West Bromwich Albion as a YTS player by Alan Buckley. To be offered a professional contract from school by a League side was one of the best moments for Tony James, the expectations of what might be. In his first season Tony James made his Pontins League debut against Liverpool at Anfield, a team he supported as a boy.

Tony spent three years with West Bromwich Albion, one of which was as a fully fledged professional, playing mainly in the Pontins League. Unfortunately, West Bromwich Albion had around forty professionals and Tony was unable to get into the first-team squad. He then went to Tranmere Rovers, again playing in the Pontins League, but was not taken on. It was Greg Downing who received a telephone call saying that Tony James was available, and he came to Edgar Street to play in some friendlies at the end of the 1997/98 season after being told that Hereford liked to play a passing game. Graham Turner signed Tony James after he had put in some good performances in the friendlies, however, he admits that his first season with the Bulls was something of a culture shock. He was surprised how much faster and more physical the game was compared to the football in the Pontins League. Tony formed a good understanding with then club captain Ian Wright at the heart of Hereford United's defence, a player Tony James has said is the best player he has played with, week in, week out. Another player Tony James rates highly is Gavin Williams, who moved to Yeovil and then West Ham after playing for Hereford United. Tony James has scored several important goals for United, very often from the penalty spot, his first goal coming away from Edgar Street against Sutton United, the first game of the 1999/2000 season. United were 1-0 down and Tony's far-post header meant that United came away with a draw.

Tony James has won the Player of the Year trophy and the Ray Mercier Memorial Trophy, presented by the *Worcester Evening News*. In June 2002 he helped Wales become the first Unibond Four Nations Semi-Pro Tournament champions, playing the full ninety minutes in all three of their games. His reward was keeping a Welsh shirt and winning a cap.

Tony has had the experience of playing against League clubs in the FA Cup, and when United played Leicester City in the third round in the 1999/2000 season he came up against Tony Cottee, an England international, for a second time. The first occasion was in a Pontins League game. Since Tony joined Hereford United they have experienced the highs and lows of football: excellent matches against League clubs in the FA Cup and LDV Vans Trophy; and the lows of losing in the Conference play-offs. The latter Tony describes as his worst moments in football, along with being unable to play for fourteen to fifteen weeks with a torn hamstring. His plans for the future include winning the Conference with Hereford United and then seeing where they go from there, as he believes that United could win promotion two seasons running. The best thing about playing for Hereford United, according to Tony James, is that as a team they are allowed to express themselves on the pitch, using their own imaginations. He hates the way that many teams come to Edgar Street to defend.

After Tony James was presented with the Herefordshire Senior Cup at the start of this season Tony said, 'Let's hope that this is an omen and at the end of the season I am lifting another trophy, as Conference winners' – a sentiment shared by all United supporters.

James defends the Hereford cause, *c.* 2001.

Alan Jones

Midfield, 1968–1974

Prior to 1972/73

	Appearances	Goals
	276	21

Football League era

	Appearances	Goals
League	52 (1)	2
Other	6	2

Previous clubs: Swansea City

Alan Jones joined from Swansea in January of the 1967/68 season after having won a Welsh Under-23 cap in 1967 when he played against England. He was born in Swansea in 1945 and played 5 times for the Welsh Schoolboys team. Alan signed for Swansea as an amateur before moving to Liverpool as an apprentice. He was only at Anfield for three months before returning to Swansea without having played a game for Liverpool. He was still registered as an amateur by Swansea and eventually it was decided by the hierarchy that Alan Jones was a Swansea player. He played 58 first-team games for Swansea, making his debut at the age of nineteen, during the 1964/65 season. He was given the job of marking Welsh international Wynn Davies in a match against Bolton Wanderers, a team that also featured a teenage Francis Lee, who went on to play for England. Alan Jones was the star of the match, which Swansea won 2-0, but Swansea went on to be relegated that season, during which Alan made only three more first-team appearances. The following season he became a first-team regular, scoring 3 goals in 26 matches. During his spell at Swansea they won the Welsh Cup for the third time in their history. He played in the European Cup-Winners' Cup against Slavia of Sofia in 1966, alongside Brian Evans, Brian Purcell and Roy Evans, who later also went on to play for Hereford United. Alas, Brian Purcell and Roy Evans were tragically killed on the Heads of the Valley road a few years later while they were United players. Alan Jones played 59 games for Swansea and played in the Welsh Under-23 side in 1967 against England, who won 8-0. John Charles signed Alan on loan in January 1968 at a time when he was not playing regular first-team football for Swansea and once said that he regarded the signing of Alan Jones as one of the best signings that he ever made. He jumped at the chance of bringing him to Edgar Street. John Charles said, 'Alan is a real professional in the true sense of the word and two of his main virtues on the playing field are his consistency and reliability, especially when Hereford are under pressure. He is a wholehearted player who puts everything into his game.' Alan made his debut against Barnet playing in the centre half position, and the crowd soon began to appreciate his talents. The move from Swansea was made permanent at the end of the season. Within a few months of arriving at Edgar Street he starred in United's 1-0 victory at Somerton Park, when Hereford United knocked Newport County out of the Welsh Cup. They won 1-0 thanks to an Albert Derrick goal that put United into the Welsh Cup final for the first time in the club's history. Alan was made club captain for the 1969/1970 season and he played in 72 out of 74 matches in that season. in 1973/74 he became only the fifth player in the history of Hereford United to make 350 first-team appearances, the milestone coming against Aldershot. He played a total of 361 competitive games for the senior side and only three other players had made more first-team appearances in the club's fifty-year history. The other three were John Layton (549 in 1964), Charlie Thompson (452 in thirteen seasons) and Reggie Bowen (438 in fourteen years). Alan Jones achieved the distinction in only six seasons, a club record, reaching the 300 mark in just over four years. He is also only one of the few players to have played for Hereford United in the Southern League and the Football League. He also scored some important goals, including one against Northampton Town in the FA Cup at Edgar Street in 1970. United were losing 2-0 when Alan scored a superb fifty-seventh-minute header and Brian Owen scored the equaliser. When Hereford United won the replay it established the club as a serious contender for a place in the Fourth Division. He was also a member of the giant-killing side who beat Newcastle United and West Ham United. In fact, in 1974, he scored the winning goal in the seventy-third minute from eighteen yards out against West Ham at Edgar Street in the replay. United gained a corner on the left and from Brian Evans' cross the ball went to Dudley Tyler who squared it to Alan, who struck a perfect shot. He had marked the Hammers' player Clyde Best out of the game and said that the goal against West Ham was the best he had ever scored. He became known as 'Mr Consistency', although a number of Hereford United fans gave Alan the nickname 'Trampas' after the star of the TV series *The Virginians*. Acker Bilk and his Jazzmen appeared at the Crystal Ballroom in aid of his testimonial, which he was granted for his outstanding achievements.

In 1974 Alan was transferred to Southport and later played for Merthyr Tydfil. After giving up football Alan became a prison officer.

Alan Judge

Goalkeeper, 1991–1994

Football League era

	Appearances	Clean sheets
League	105	17
Other	15	9

Previous clubs: Luton Town, Reading, Oxford United

Alan Judge was a goalkeeper who won the hearts of Hereford United and Oxford United supporters with his many fine acrobatic saves. He was born in Kingsbury on 15 May 1960 and was a junior with Luton Town before being offered full professional terms in January 1978. After making 11 first-team appearances for the Hatters he went out on loan to Reading, where he made 33 appearances during an extended loan period. Following his many fine performances, it came as no surprise when Reading made his move permanent in September 1982. After 44 more appearances, Alan moved to the Manor Ground, and he eventually won a League Cup medal with them in 1985/86. They beat Queens Park Rangers 3-0 at Wembley, with Alan making some crucial saves in the second half after John Aldridge had put Oxford in front five minutes before half-time. After Hebberd had split the QPR defence, Houghton ran through and scored a second before Charles made sure of Oxford lifting the trophy by scoring their third goal four minutes before the end of the match. Alan was also a vital member of the team that reached the First Division but was unable to halt their slide back down to the lower divisions. He made 80 appearances for Oxford United but was unable to maintain a regular position in the team, going out on loan to Lincoln City where he made 2 League appearances in 1985/86, and to Cardiff City in 1987/88, where he made 8 League appearances.

During the summer of 1991 John Sillett obtained the signature of Alan Judge, but it was not until 6 November that he made his debut for the Bulls against Halifax Town. He took the place of Tony Elliott, who had the unfortunate distinction of being a goalkeeper who had let an opposing goalkeeper, Ian Hesford, score against him in a match that United lost 3-2 at Maidstone! Alan was the third person to wear the goalkeeper's jersey that season, as Kevin Rose had started the season in goal. Alan soon won the support of the Edgar Street supporters with his acrobatic one-handed saves; with the United defence under pressure, many felt that it was down to him that United did not slip to the bottom of the Football League and thus saved them from the embarrassment of relegation. There was very little money in the bank and Hereford United were unable to spend on players. Instead they had to be content with making savings where possible. United finished up in seventeenth place that season, having conceded 56 goals, and only managing to score 45. Alan had made 24 appearances for the Bulls that season and was the only ever-present team member the following season, when he was awarded the Player of the Year trophy by Hereford United supporters' clubs around the county. When supporters heard that Alan was considering retiring from full-time League football they encouraged him to stay at Edgar Street, with shouts of 'Judge must stay' as he collected his trophies. The United defence had let in 60 League goals that season and the team again finished in seventeenth place, having scored 47 goals. Alan remained with Hereford United for another season instead of helping out running his family business, making 39 League appearances. This time Hereford United finished in twentieth place, having let in 79 goals, although this season the team did manage to score 60.

It was still a major surprise when Alan made the decision to go part-time at the end of the 1993/94 season. If he had one weakness it was his dead-ball kicking and he did not appear to be comfortable with the new rule regarding the handling of back passes. However, he was soon signed up by Bromsgrove Rovers, who played in the GM Vauxhall Conference, and the future England manager Glenn Hoddle, then manager of Chelsea, also signed him as a non-contract player as cover for European matches. As there was a limit on imported players that were allowed to feature in a team line-up at any one time, he did actually appear on the bench for Chelsea. Alan moved to Kettering Town for a while before returning to Oxford United. Despite going into retirement from football for a short time he was persuaded to return and signed for Swindon Town before making a return to Oxford United, where he made a first-team appearance in 2004/05.

Alan will be best remembered for his consistent goalkeeping and the steadying influence he had on the Hereford United defence. He made some crucial saves and became a firm favourite with the Edgar Street fans, making a total of 105 League appearances for the Bulls.

Mick McLaughlin

Defender, 1970–1975

Prior to 1972/73

	Appearances	Goals
	117	

Football League era

	Appearances	Goals
League	84	1
Other	7	

Previous clubs: Newport County, Merthyr Tydfil, Barry Town, Lovells Athletic

Mick McLaughlin was signed from Newport County in 1970. Along with Alan Jones he went on to form a defence that was to concede fewer goals, only 30, in a season than ever before achieved by a Southern League Premier team.

He was born in Newport in January 1943 and played local football until being spotted by Newport County, for whom he signed as a professional in November 1961. Newport County, however, were relegated at the end of the 1961/62 season after finishing bottom of the League with just seven victories from forty-six matches, during which Mick played fourteen matches at the heart of their defence. That defence let 102 goals in that season and changes meant that Mick was released by Newport County and went back to playing non-League football. He played for Merthyr Tydfil before playing for Barry Town and then Lovells Athletic in the Southern League. During these five years Mick McLaughlin built up a great reputation as a brilliant defender who had top leadership qualities, so much so that Newport County persuaded him to re-sign for them as a centre half in August 1968. During the 1968/69 and 1969/70 season he made 90 appearances for Newport County, missing only two matches in two seasons, In August 1970 John Charles brought Mick McLaughlin to join the Bulls as club captain as they pressed for promotion to the Football League. His first competitive match for United was against Barnet at Underhill Road in the Southern League Premier Division, on 15 August 1970, when Hereford United won 2-0 with goals from Dudley Tyler and Billy Meadows. This was Hereford United's first ever win at Barnet. Ironically, Mick was not allowed to be captain for that game, that job going to Billy Meadows, who also made his debut for United on that day, and as he had been signed from Barnet, the privilege went to him. During the season Hereford lost only 5 of their first 26 Premier Division matches, but their involvement in cup competitions and bad weather conditions meant that thirteen League matches had to be played in just twenty-eight days to complete their League fixtures. Hereford United finished fourth in the League; however, cup victories included wins against Kidderminster Harriers 5-0 and Northampton Town 2-1 (after a 2-2 draw at Edgar Street, before being beaten by Brighton 2-1 in the second round). During the Bulls' famous cup run of the 1971/72 season Mick McLaughlin was club captain and he became Hereford United's first club captain in the Football League after their promotion. He made 208 first-team appearances for the Bulls and scored one goal against Hartlepool. He dived headlong to net a stunning goal, the only goal scored in a 1-0 victory for the Bulls at the Victoria Ground. It was the first goal that goalkeeper Barry Watling had conceded in 566 minutes' play. Mick was deputising in midfield for the suspended Harry Gregory for the duration of this match in March 1973. The following year, when United were in the Third Division, Mick snapped his Achilles tendon when playing Walsall away from home in the final match of the season. He returned after an eleven-month lay-off in February 1975, but only made a further eight appearances for the Bulls before leaving Edgar Street. Mick returned to Newport County on a non-contract basis after leaving Hereford United but only played seven more times for them. He also turned his attention to rugby for a short while, appearing for Newport Saracens RFC, before moving to Atlanta, Georgia, in the United States of America, but Mick still found time for Hereford United by returning to Edgar Street as part of the Giant-killers XI, and indeed kept in touch with his former teammates.

His robust tackling and never-say-die attitude will be long remembered by the older generation of Hereford United fans, as will his ability to captain a football team. He always led by example, something players of today would do well to emulate. His was always able to read the game and often saved the Bulls when his last-ditch tackles prevented the opposition from scoring a goal. One of the more humorous reasons some supporters will remember Mick is when he changed his shorts and jockstrap while in full view of the Merton Grandstand. During his time at Hereford United Football Club he played arguably some of his best football, with many of his fans feeling that he was unlucky not to be selected to play for his home international team of Wales.

Directing operations on the Hereford United training ground.

Dixie McNeil

Striker, 1974–1977, 1982

Football League era

	Appearances	Goals
League	140 (1)	88
Other	19	6

Previous clubs: Holywell Works, Leicester City, Exeter City, Corby Town, Northampton Town, Lincoln City

While the name of Hereford United may always be associated with the FA Cup and the giant-killing of Newcastle and West Ham, there are very many people who will only remember one player, Dixie McNeil. Without doubt he was the striker supreme and one of the best to ever play at Edgar Street. He will always be remembered for the numerous wonderful goals that he scored for Hereford United. His dazzling displays on the hallowed turf of Edgar Street will be revered for many years to come by the faithful. Dixie was born in Melton Mowbray, Leicestershire, in January 1944 and he played his early football for the local League side Holwell Works before being spotted by Leicester City in December 1964. He played many games for Leicester City reserves during the eighteen months he was there before joining Exeter City in June 1966, for whom he made his League debut later that year. He scored 11 goals in 31 appearances but was surprisingly released. After joining Corby Town in the Southern League he scored so frequently that he was signed by Northampton Town in May 1969, thus rejoining the Football League. Dixie scored for Northampton Town against Hereford United in the FA Cup in 1970 and scored 33 goals in total for Northampton Town in 85 games before moving to Lincoln City in January 1972 for a fee of £15,000. His goal-scoring record improved again, here he scored 53 goals in 97 matches. He already had an awesome goal-scoring reputation but when John Sillett brought Dixie McNeil to Edgar Street for a bargain £20,000 (a club record) from Lincoln City in 1974 few could have realised the impact he would have for the team, the fans and the club. Dixie scored six goals in a pre-season friendly win over a Gibraltar FA XI, with Brian Evans scoring four as well. Dixie also scored on his debut for the club in a 2-0 win against Aldershot on the opening day of the 1974/75 season. He made an immediate impact and he was the Football League top scorer with 31 goals, 9 of them penalties, in 44 matches. Again, the following season he was top scorer of the entire Football League and his goals helped Hereford United to be promoted to the Second Division in 1975/76. Top marksman at the club three seasons running and voted Player of the Year in 1975, he was always going to score a goal. He scored 87 goals for the club

Dixie McNeil

Striker, 1974–1977, 1982

McNeil beats the goalkeeper and scores for Hereford United.

in 180 League and cup appearances. Dixie was the first player to score a hat-trick for the club and four goals in a match since United had joined the Football League. In all, Dixie netted five hat-tricks during his spell at Edgar Street in matches against Burnley, Chester, Blackburn Rovers, Chesterfield and Preston North End. The 6-3 win against Blackburn Rovers was against a side that had only conceded seventeen goals in twenty-one matches prior to that against Hereford United. They still recovered to win the championship and their defeat against Hereford was the heaviest in that campaign. In the 1974/75 season Dixie was awarded a special Rothmans plaque for his goal-scoring activities and contribution to the wide spectrum of the game. He was one of only half a dozen soccer personalities to be honoured by Rothmans and shared the accolade with Fulham's skipper Alan Mullery, West Ham's two-goal cup final hero Alan Taylor, Derby County's Colin Todd, Wimbledon goalkeeper Dickie Guy and Welsh team manager Mike Smith. He was also voted the best centre forward in the Third Division by fellow players, when the Professional Footballers Association held their awards dinner at the London Hilton Hotel. In the 1975/76 season he scored a record 35 goals in 40 appearances and became Hereford United's highest goal scorer in a season at that point. His partnership with Steve Davey, who also scored 18 League goals that season, was easily the most prolific since

McNeil calls for the vital pass.

United had joined the Football League. Dixie went into the final match of the season against Preston North End, needing a hat-trick to finish once again top goal-scorer in the country. In a match that also saw the League debut of young starlet Kevin Sheedy, United won 3-1 with Dixie duly scoring his hat-trick. In the Second Division, things were a lot tougher, but Dixie McNeil still managed to score 16 goals. There are a number of fans who believed that if he had played with players of a higher calibre he could have scored goals in the highest League. With a below-average start to the 1977/78 season Dixie McNeil moved to Wrexham in September 1977, following United's relegation from the Second Division and their poor financial position, for £60,000. His three goals scored before his transfer made him the Bulls' top goal-scorer right up to January, such was the scarcity of goals for United. His wonderful partnership with Steve Davey had come to an end. Despite large attendances at Edgar Street the previous season, United had been living beyond their means and the transfer money was very welcome. He was an instant success at Wrexham and Dixie enjoyed great popularity, although scoring fewer goals. He formed a formidable partnership with Graham Whittle and Bobby Shinton. Wrexham had only won 1 game out of 7, the same as Hereford United, when they bought Dixie, but they went on to win the championship that season. He set an FA Cup record for Wrexham by scoring in ten consecutive rounds. He even played in Europe, in the Cup-Winners' Cup, following Wrexham's victory in the Welsh Cup. Dixie made a brief return to Edgar Street in 1982 where he scored 3 times in 12 games. United won the first game that Dixie played in 1-0 against Crewe, and this was their first win in ten games that season. They also won their next match and those six points lifted United off the foot of the table, but the fans' jubilation was short-lived as they only managed 1 win in the next 8 matches. Dixie's return could not work miracles; with his thirty-eighth birthday fast approaching, he was no longer able to meet the high standards he set himself on the pitch. He became manager for a while at Chirk before returning to the Racecourse as manager of Wrexham. A coaching role followed at Coventry City before he left the world of football, after which Dixie went on to work at the Marstons brewery. In an illustrious football career Dixie McNeil scored 239 League goals in 522 appearances while at five football clubs. It was once said that Dixie could score goals with any part of his anatomy, one even appearing to go in off the palm of his hand against Shrewsbury, but off the pitch he was well known for his pleasantness and good manners.

McNeil practises his heading.

Gavin Mahon

Midfield, 1997–1998

Football League era

	Appearances	Goals
League	10 (1)	1
Other	4	0

Conference era

	Appearances	Goals
League	59	3
Other	9	0

Previous clubs: Wolverhampton Wanderers

Although the 1996/97 season will be remembered by Hereford United fans for all the wrong reasons, as it was the season they were finally relegated from the Football League after twenty-five years, it was also the season that saw the arrival of Gavin Mahon at Edgar Street. Although when he first made his appearance at Edgar Street there were a few supporters who thought that this time manager Graham Turner had got it wrong, Gavin went on to prove his critics wrong, and he is now playing for Watford.

Gavin Andrew Mahon was born in Birmingham in January 1977 and supported Birmingham City as a boy. He joined Wolverhampton Wanderers straight from school in 1995, but did not make any first-team appearances for them. He did play regularly for their reserve team in the Pontins League, but was released when a new regime took over at the Molineux club. Moving to Edgar Street in the summer of 1996, the midfield player made his League debut for the Bulls away at Fulham in the first League game of the season, and a week later made his debut at Edgar Street. He joined a young and inexperienced team; many of the stars of the previous season's outfit that got through to the Division Three play-offs had left. Hereford United were unable to match the offers from other League clubs. The books had to be balanced, Graham Turner having inherited a club heavily in debt, but he later admitted that he would have loved to have retained a few more players. He publicly praised his squad, stating that he could never recall working with a better bunch of players in terms of attitude and honesty. He felt that his young squad could only improve. One of the highlights of Gavin's career while with Hereford was playing against Middlesbrough in the League Cup, even though United lost 7-0. His first League goal was scored at Edgar Street in a 3-0 victory against Rochdale. His opening goal was followed by goals from Chris Hargreaves and Adrian Foster. Apparently Gavin liked to moan a lot and this earned him the nickname of 'Victor' from his fellow team-mates, after Victor Meldrew of the television sitcom, *One Foot in the Grave*. Although he was primarily a midfielder, Gavin was a utility player who could play in almost any position in a football team. Gavin made a total of 15 appearances for the club in his first season, scoring just the one goal, but the following season he started to show his great ability on the football pitch. He made the number eleven shirt his by right, and was rewarded for his consistency and skill by being voted Player of the Season after having been regularly voted 'Player of the Month'. The following season Gavin made 17 appearances and scored 3 goals for Hereford United, and made his final appearance for the Bulls away at Leek Town, before moving to Brentford on 16 November 1998 for a £50,000 fee. He made his first League appearance for the Bees away at Leyton Orient on 21 November when they suffered a 2-0 defeat, but they went on to be Division Three champions that season under Micky Adams. Gavin continued to exhibit all the skills that he had shown at Edgar Street, and made 29 League appearances for Brentford, scoring 4 goals in the remainder of the 1998/99 season. He stayed with the Griffin Park club until 4 March 2002 and made 141 appearances for the club, scoring 8 goals.

In March 2002 Gavin moved to Watford for a fee of £150,000, when Gianluca Vialli was manager. He made his debut for the Hornets on 9 March 2002 away at Crystal Palace, and made a total of 6 appearances for Watford during the last couple of months of the season. The Vicarage Road club were FA Cup semi-finalists in 2003. Gavin again showed his great football ability for the Hornets, and was rewarded for his endeavours by winning the Player of the Year award in the 2003/04 season for Watford. In 2004/05 he was made team captain in place of the injured Sean Dyche, and made 43 League appearances. One of the highlights of his career to date has been reaching the semi-finals of the Carling Cup, when the Vicarage Road club were drawn against Liverpool. He turned in an outstanding performance in the away leg at Anfield when they lost 1-0. Liverpool played Chelsea in the final at the Millennium Stadium, when they lost 3-2. Gavin is a player who wins over the fans wherever he plays. His high level of consistency will ensure that we will hear more of this player in the future.

Ken Mallender

Defender, 1971–1974

Prior to 1972/73

	Appearances	Goals
	80	

Football League era

	Appearances	Goals
League	71	1
Other	1	

Previous clubs: Sheffield United, Norwich City

Ken Mallender was a great character with a very infectious laugh who used to cheer everyone up in the dressing room at Edgar Street. Billy Meadows and Ricky George used to do cockney impersonations, Blakey from *On the Buses* and Alf Garnett from *Till Death Us Do Part*, a few words from them would start Ken off and his laughter used to start everyone else off. He became known as the 'laughing policeman'.

He was born at Thrybergh in South Yorkshire in December 1943 and was first spotted playing in local football before being snapped up by Sheffield United. He joined the Blades on apprentice forms before signing as a professional in February 1961. He made a total of 144 appearances for Sheffield United during the next seven seasons, as a full-back, scoring 2 goals. Sheffield United were a First Division club at this point and during Ken's spell at Sheffield they were one of the top ten clubs in the country, only finishing lower (nineteenth) in the 1964/65 season. Ken names the Sheffield local derbies as one of the highlights of his career; they were keenly fought contests in front of passionate crowds to whom a win was all-important, both clubs fighting for supremacy in the city. In December 1967 Colin Addison joined Sheffield United from Arsenal, which was to be significant for Ken Mallender later on.

Following the relegation of Sheffield United at the end of the previous season, Ken transferred to Norwich City in October 1968 for £45,000, where he made 46 appearances in his eighteen-month spell at Carrow Road for the Canaries. He left Norwich in 1971 on a free transfer and joined Hereford United, who were playing in the Southern League at the time. This was a popular signing as Ken was only twenty-seven and there were many who thought that he was good enough to be playing in the Football League. This signing brought back the partnership of Ken and Colin Addison, who joined shortly after.

Ken was a firm favourite with the Edgar Street crowd and even more so when his late equaliser against Northampton Town in the second replay at The Hawthorns brought extra time in the second round of the giant-killing FA Cup run in 1971/72. By the time of the second replay United knew their destination in the third round, an away trip to St James' Park, home of Newcastle United, one of the most famous football clubs in the country. What an incentive to win a match, a mouth-watering fixture against the likes of

Malcolm Macdonald, but it was the same for both clubs. Over 6,000 fans made their way up the M5 to make up the bulk of the 8,331 spectators at The Hawthorns. Hereford United were 1-0 down at half-time thanks to a goal scored by the Cobblers centre forward Large. He had also scored in the 2-2 draw, along with Hawkins, Dudley Tyler and Brian Owen scoring for Hereford. The Bulls attacked for practically all of the second half, Ricky George having two shots cleared off the line, with Hereford United fans frantically cheering the team on. The ninety minutes were up when the ball came out to Ken Mallender on the edge of the penalty area. He drove it back in, first time along the ground, and it whistled into the back of the net. He sprinted the whole fifty yards back to the halfway line with the whole team in pursuit! Northampton kicked off and the referee blew his whistle for full time. Dudley Tyler scored the winner in extra time after Mallender's twenty-yard cracker. The famous games against Newcastle and West Ham followed, which catapulted Hereford United into the history books. Ken names the matches against Northampton Town, Newcastle United and West Ham United as the most satisfying of his career.

He played a total of 154 games for Hereford United and only missed one game for the Bulls in the Fourth Division during the 1972/73 season. Ken was a hard-tackling defender who loved to indulge in banter with the Edgar Street fans along the terracing on the side of the ground. The only Football League goal he scored for Hereford United was against Halifax at The Shay in the 1973/74 season.

Ken later played for Minehead, Telford United and Llandrindod Wells, while maintaining links with United, and has played at Edgar Street for the Giant-killing XI and in benefit matches. He also became player coach at Telford United.

He later joined M & M Sports, who help supply kit for the Bulls and sponsor the team.

Dudley Tyler and Ken Mallender celebrate the victory over Newcastle, 5 February 1972.

Billy Meadows

Striker, 1970–1972

Prior to 1972/73

	Appearances	Goals
	104	47

Previous clubs: Arsenal, Dunstable, Hillingdon Borough, Hastings, Barnet

William Mark Meadows started his career at Arsenal, playing wing half in the 'A' team. He scored eight goals in the 13-0 win over Dunstable Town and was then dropped for being greedy! On leaving Arsenal he played for a number of non-League clubs including Dunstable, Hillingdon and Hastings. At every club he scored lots of goals, although he wasn't tall at five feet nine inches and had no pace. He had also broken his nose half a dozen times challenging centre halves and goalkeepers. An early cartilage operation while at Hastings United in the 1967/68 season had left him with a slight limp and his front teeth were missing. However, he gained a formidable reputation for a superb left foot and his brilliance in the air. It was at Hastings that he met up with Ricky George, and they played alongside each other for three seasons, before both moving on to Barnet. Ricky George described Billy Meadows as one of the most natural of goal-scorers. He scored a remarkable 72 goals at Barnet, making him a hero. He hit a hat-trick for them in a 4-1 London Challenge Cup win against an Arsenal side that included George Graham, George Armstrong, Pat Rice and Sammy Nelson. Other players at Barnet had nicknamed Billy Meadows 'Bill the Shoot'.

When Billy Meadows asked Barnet for a pay rise as a reward for his endeavours the club refused his demand for an extra £5 per week, and he was sold to Hereford United for £300. Arguably one of the best signings ever made at Edgar Street, Billy Meadows was signed for Hereford United by player-manager John Charles at the start of the 1970/71 season and he scored 24 goals in each of his two seasons with the club. He relished playing under John Charles and once described his life at Edgar Street thus, 'Great guy, great bunch of lads, terrific team, fantastic supporters.' It was Billy Meadows who encouraged Ricky George to leave Underhill Road and move to Hereford, saying that the supporters at Edgar Street were as good as a twelfth man. The atmosphere at Edgar Street was described as being like nowhere else in non-League football. 'The ground always looked full, with 5,000 or so spectators for every home game.'

Billy Meadows scored on his debut in the sixth minute on the opening day of the 1970/71 season, when he returned to Underhill Road, Barnet's ground, with Dudley Tyler scoring another to give United a well-deserved victory.

Billy Meadows

Striker, 1970–1972

Some of the Barnet supporters were calling him 'a traitor', as Billy Meadows had been made Hereford United's club captain prior to that game. In the same season Ricky George scored a hat-trick for Barnet in the first round of the FA Cup against Newport County, Barnet winning 6-1. In the Newport side was a midfielder by the name of Ron Radford. Ricky George eventually joined Hereford United but Billy and Ricky never trained at Edgar Street. Part of the deal was that they trained at Underhill Road instead.

Billy had gained an England Youth cap against Wales in 1959 and his thirty-five-yard strike against Kettering at Edgar Street on 14 November 1970 was one of his favourite goals. Another memorable moment was when he scored United's only goal in the FA Cup replay at Upton Park against West Ham after Geoff Hurst had scored a hat-trick. This goal generated more noise than those of Hurst, even though thousands of United fans were locked out at Upton Park that day. The Hereford United team had to be escorted to Upton Park, the coach being stuck behind the coaches carrying Hereford United supporters. The team even had to walk the last 200 yards, with the skip containing the players' kit being laid across two motorcycles. There were supporters on sky-scraper blocks and roof-tops, perching wherever they could. United fans who were locked out of the match were kept informed of what was happening in the ground by the supporters who managed to see the match.

Billy Meadows made 104 appearances for the Bulls, scoring 47 goals. His last game for United was against Margate in the Southern League on 29 April 1972. He wanted to remain part-time and Hereford United made the decision to turn professional once they were elected to the Football League. Billy Meadows returned to Underhill Road to play for Barnet and then played for AOS Ostende for a while. He returned to Barnet as manager for the 1975/76 season, with Barnet gaining promotion in his first full season as manager, signing Jimmy Greaves and Terry Mancini. Billy Meadows has since returned to Edgar Street to play in charity and benefit matches, and the 'giant-killers' have enjoyed many reunions.

Tamika Mkandawire

Defender, 2003–

Conference era

	Appearances	Goals
League	47 (11)	5
Other	11	3

Previous clubs: West Bromwich Albion

Tamika Mkandawire is a central defender who has won the admiration of the Bulls' fans in a very short time. In his first full season with Hereford United he won the Player of the Year award and the HUISA away travel Player of the Year trophy.

Although Tamika was born in Malawi on 28 May 1983, he has no early recollections of that country as he moved to England when he was only a year old. His father had lived in Malawi all his life, but his mother is from Rugby, which is where they now live. Tamika played his first game of football for a local Sunday League side when he was nine years old and, from then on, to quote him, 'I was hooked.' During the next five years he played football all over Warwickshire with his school and club team, and came to realise the enjoyment of playing a team sport. He learnt how to savour success and handle defeat, and made some great friends along the way. As Tamika was quite tall for his age he was usually put in defence, even though he would have preferred to play up front or in midfield. This changed as he got older and he managed to play in virtually every position on the pitch, centre midfield being the position he favoured most.

Although he very much enjoyed playing football, he did not really seriously consider it as a professional career until he was fifteen years old. Having decided he would like to carry on playing football he wrote to seven football clubs in the West Midlands and, although West Bromwich Albion were his least favourite, they were the team that sent scouts to watch Tamika. Within weeks he was training with their Under-16s. Tamika was at The Hawthorns as an apprentice for three years, at the end of which he was offered a professional contract for two years with the option of a further year. During his first season as a professional Tamika trained and travelled with the first-team squad, but was never given the opportunity to prove himself. There was no improvement in his second year, when he was not always given a game in the reserves.

Tamika said: 'However, there was light at the end of the tunnel! Hereford United came in for me on loan and gave me the chance to play first-team football for three months.' His debut for the Bulls was away at Woking on 4 October 2003. Tamika was brought to Edgar Street as cover for the injured Andy Tretton. This was the break that Tamika needed, the football club steeped in tradition gave Tamika a very warm welcome and provided him with a new challenge. That season he made 18 appearances for the Bulls, in two loan spells, scoring 1 goal in the eighty-ninth minute at Gay Meadow. In one of Hereford United's worst performances of the season, they were beaten 4-1 by Shrewsbury.

Tamika left West Bromwich Albion after his second season as a professional, because it was made very clear to him that he would not be involved in the plans of the first team. With his pace and skill with the ball contributing to some very impressive displays from Tamika, United gave him the chance to enjoy first-team football in a supportive environment by offering him a one-year contract. During the 2004/05 season Tamika really started to turn in some great displays in 41 full appearances for the Bulls, winning the Man of the Match award on numerous occasions. He scored 7 goals, most of them headers from set pieces, and helped the team to reach the play-off semi-finals for the second year running. Although the Bulls failed in their attempt to win promotion, Tamika had a very successful season and feels very optimistic about the future. His skills on the football pitch have won him a lot of fans, and this is why he was nominated for the *Non-League Paper* team of the season, and the reason for winning the awards at Edgar Street. His style of play and ability to read the game make him a very sound defender who does not need to resort to dirty tackles. The future looks very bright for this young footballer. We all hope that he gets a chance to play in the Football League, preferably with Hereford United. One of the most amusing features of travelling to away matches is listening to the Public Address officials reading out the away team list! Tamika was recently rewarded for his outstanding ability by being picked for the England National game XI, who played Belgium in the first ever non-League European Championship in Brussels.

Adam Musial

Defender/midfield, 1980–1983

Football League era

	Appearances	Goals
League	44 (2)	
Other	2	

Previous clubs: Arka Gydnia

On 17 October 1973 England played Poland at Wembley stadium in a vital World Cup qualifier. The target for the English players was simple: they had to win, while their opponents needed only to draw to reach the World Cup finals due to be held in West Germany the following summer. The previous meeting, which had taken place in June of that year, resulted in a shock 2-0 win for Poland. Those who saw the game, either by being there or watching it on television, have never forgotten it as they witnessed one of the most remarkable games of football that ever took place. From the onset, England attacked the Polish team but failed to score enough goals to win, the match ending in a 1-1 draw. There were many heroes of the Polish team that night. Poland defended as if their lives depended on it and, although the goalkeeper Jan Tomaszewski took the credit, making some outstanding and often lucky saves despite being labelled 'a clown' by Brian Clough, one of the many other heroes was Adam Musial the full-back. At the time, none of the Polish team were household names to most British football fans. At the end of the night many people could not forget them. By the end of the 1974 World Cup finals the Polish team was known to many football fans all over the world.

Adam Musial joined Hereford in 1980 after going on from that glorious night at Wembley to represent his country at the 1974 World Cup finals where they surprised many, finishing third after beating some of the favourites such as Italy and Argentina. When it was announced that Hereford had signed a former Polish international, many fans were asking: 'Who is Adam Musial?' Others perhaps remembered his name from that night at Wembley and perhaps considered this to be a shrewd signing. His record was comparable to many of the foreign players who were joining British clubs at that time. He had gained 34 caps for his country, played three games in the World Cup finals, which included the third-place play-off, and had gained a wealth of experience playing in some of the most hostile arenas of world football. No doubt he found Hereford United completely different from his previous club, Arka Gydnia.

Adam Musial

Defender/midfield, 1980–1983

Signed by the then-manager Frank Lord, his League debut for the club was inconspicuous and he seemed out of touch with the football being played. Some fans felt his defending left a lot to be desired. Tommy Hughes, the goalkeeper, needed to take time out to explain where he wanted him to stand during the taking of corners. The visitors on that occasion were Tranmere Rovers, the game ending in a 1-1 draw. In all, Adam made 16 League appearances for the club during the season but failed to score.

Adam did not represent Hereford United during the 1981/82 season until he gained a shock recall to the team on Saturday 23 January 1982 for a FA Cup tie against Leicester City. Playing in midfield, this was arguably his best ever game in a United shirt. Having earned a surprise recall, Adam helped an inspired Hereford team as they valiantly fought to overcome a First Division team. Losing 1-0, Hereford almost equalised near the end when an exciting run from Musial needed desperate defending by Leicester to keep the score intact.

During the 1982/83 season Adam made 4 League appearances before leaving the club, a decision necessary in order to prevent the loss of his home if he chose to stay in England. Adam Musial was known to have been disappointed at the prospect of not playing for Hereford United again. Many of the fans of the period were sorry to see him leave and retain fond memories of a quality player who, sadly, despite his best efforts, failed to live up to the high standard he had achieved in his younger days.

Musial in action.

Tommy Naylor

Defender, 1972–1974

Football League era

	Appearances	Goals
League	73 (2)	4
Other	8	1

Previous clubs: Bournemouth

Another of the important signings made by Colin Addison to strengthen and improve his squad for the club's first tilt at League football was Tommy Naylor, who joined the club in August 1972. Born in Blackburn in April 1946, the former Bournemouth player had made 139 appearances for his former club, scoring 3 goals. He had been signed on as an apprentice as soon as he had left school, with many other League clubs interested in signing him. He started out as an inside left before changing to the left-back position, where his sound tackling and distribution skills became a trademark of his play. Tommy was offered a full professional contract at Dean Court in October 1963 and, after two seasons playing for their reserves, Tommy made his debut in the 1964/65 season. By the age of twenty-one Tommy had already made 50 appearances for the Cherries and he quickly built up a reputation as a reliable defender. With experience, Tommy started to instigate many attacks with his overlapping style of play, a feature that was to thrill United fans in the future. In ten years playing for Bournemouth, Tommy made 142 appearances up to May 1972, before being persuaded to join the Bulls by Colin Addison for their first season in the Football League. Making his League debut for Hereford United in the away defeat at Colchester, Tommy Naylor made 35 appearances at full-back during the history-making first season. He built up a great understanding with Ken Mallender and David Icke, keeping a record of 22 clean sheets. Tommy only missed eight games that season through injury and suspension. His strong, sound defending was an asset to the club as the season progressed. However, he failed to score a goal during the campaign. The following season Tommy put that right, scoring 4 goals in the League and 1 in the FA Cup, all of them penalty kicks. Perhaps the most vital goal that Tommy ever scored for the club, and most pleasing on a personal note, occurred on Wednesday 9 January 1973 in the FA Cup replay against West Ham United at Edgar Street. Home victories against Torquay United and Walton & Hersham had put Hereford United into the third round. A crowd of over 23,000 saw the third-round tie at Upton Park end in a thrilling 1-1 draw, which resulted in the replay. Before a large crowd of over 17,000 and BBC television cameras, Hereford had fallen behind to a Clyde Best goal in the thirty-third minute.

Two minutes later the chance of an equaliser came when referee Wallace awarded Hereford United a penalty. Before a hushed but expectant crowd Tommy Naylor placed the ball on the penalty spot, turned, walked away, turned again, ran forward and placed the penalty kick firmly past the Hammers' helpless goalkeeper Mervyn Day. The fans were jubilant when Alan Jones scored United's second goal to gain revenge for the defeat at the hands of West Ham two seasons earlier. The celebrations of the football team and their jubilant fans will remain forever written into the history books.

His first goal had come on Saturday 29 December 1973 in a home fixture against Charlton Athletic, a fiftieth-minute penalty in a 2-3 defeat. His next two league goals were against Grimsby Town at home on 19 January 1974 and against his former club Bournemouth away on 2 March 1974. No doubt putting away a penalty against his former club gave him tremendous satisfaction.

Tommy's final goal for the club came on Saturday 20 April 1974 at home against Chesterfield. Hereford had been a goal down since the tenth minute when substitute Eric Redrobe made an immediate impact when coming on, Hereford gaining a penalty soon after. Naylor dispatched the spot kick in his usual confident style in the sixty-fifth minute. The winner came from Redrobe in the seventy-sixth minute. With a new manager for the start of the 1974/75 season Tommy Naylor made only 2 appearances for Hereford, both away and both resulting in defeat, the opponents being Charlton Athletic and Walsall. He became player-manager of Dorchester Town in the Southern League after being released by United. One can only hope that Tommy Naylor enjoyed his time with Hereford United. His sound defending and ability to score vital penalties are well remembered by the many fans who saw him play. His no-nonsense style of play earned him the Man of the Match accolade several times for United and his darting, overlapping runs will long be remembered.

Naylor in action.

Brian Owen

Striker, 1970–1974

Prior to 1972/73

	Appearances	Goals
	88	36

Football League era

	Appearances	Goals
League	46 (11)	13
Other	4 (3)	1

Previous clubs: Welton Rovers, Weston-super-Mare, Bath City

One defender once said that trying to tackle Brian Owen was like tackling an iron bar. He was born in Bath in 1945 and played local football with Welton Rovers until the age of twenty-three while living in Wiltshire, before joining Weston-super-Mare on a part-time basis. He combined his football career with being a sales representative for the Electricity Board. After two seasons he moved to Bath City, whom he had turned down an offer from at the age of fifteen. At Twerton Park Brian was top scorer in the 1968/69 season, scoring a total of 34 goals.

Brian was signed for Hereford United from Bath during the 1970/71 season by manager John Charles. He made his debut in the League against Dartford at Edgar Street in September and netted a second-half goal to secure a 4-3 victory in front of a crowd of over 4,100.

He scored in the 2-1 win over Northampton Town in 1970, the first League side to be beaten by Hereford United in the FA Cup on a League ground in fourteen previous visits, Billy Meadows scoring the other goal. Billy in fact set up the goal for Owen as he ran on to a header from Billy to nod the ball home, just inside the goalpost. Prior to that match Hereford United had beaten Kidderminster Harriers 5-0 in the previous round when Brian Owen scored in the eighth minute and again in the twenty-eighth minute after breaking clear and racing down the centre of the pitch to claim a fine solo goal. It was in this match that Billy Meadows scored a hat-trick. In the first FA Cup match against Northampton Town at Edgar Street Brian Owen scored a memorable equaliser with just three minutes to go in front of a crowd of 10,401, latching on to a Rodgerson free-kick in a crowded goalmouth to hammer the ball home. This set up the memorable replay at the County Ground. Another of his most memorable goals was that scored at St James' Park, the home of Newcastle United, in front of a crowd of over 39,000, in January 1972. The ball from the kick-off went back to Alan Jones, who struck a long ball down the pitch that just skimmed the opposition's Pat Howard's head, and fell into the path of Brian Owen. Without halting his stride he volleyed the ball with his right foot into the top right-hand corner of the goal, past their goalkeeper McFaul. The sensational goal from Brian Owen was timed at seventeen seconds. Malcolm Macdonald equalised with a penalty after he had been brought down in the penalty area, and this was followed up by a goal from John Tudor, giving the home team the lead. But within two minutes the Bulls' player-manager Colin Addison had equalised when he scored from twenty-five yards out. Hereford United held on for a 2-2 draw and brought the First Division team to Edgar Street for a replay. The rest, as they say, is history.

Brian Owen had a fantastic partnership with Billy Meadows and they helped take the club into the Football League. He remained a part-timer and finished top scorer in United's first season in the League, having scored 11 goals in 31 appearances, even though he had chosen not to sign professional forms. His long, surging runs were always going to cause defenders problems, and he scored some brilliant goals in the Fourth Division. He was continually chasing what looked like lost causes, and his persistence as well as running at defences gave him many goal-scoring opportunities. He was very alert and seized any opportunity to capitalise on any mistakes made by defenders. One such opportunity came while playing in the Third Division. After a bad back pass by a Peterborough United defender on his home patch, Brian duly lobbed their goalkeeper to ensure United returned home with a share of the spoils. He made 15 appearances for United in the Third Division, scoring 3 goals, one of which was in the FA Cup against Torquay United. The match was played at Edgar Street and United won 3-1. The two League goals were scored against the same football club, Port Vale, one in the away game in October and the other back at Edgar Street in the following February. This goal on home territory was Brian's fiftieth goal in 150 matches. His hard work and determination won him many fans and his enthusiasm was greater than that of many full-time professional footballers. Brian Owen went on to play for Weymouth after leaving Hereford United and then returned to play for Bath City.

Owen looks for a goal, *c.* 1971.

Terry Paine

Midfield, 1974–1977

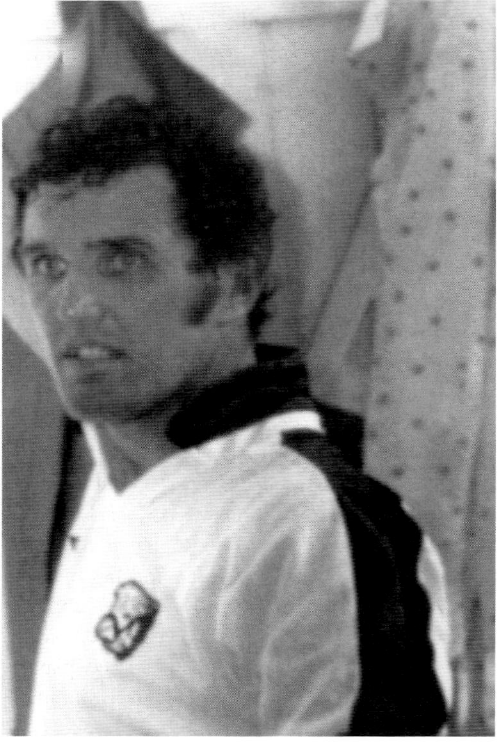

Football League era

	Appearances	Goals
League	106 (5)	8
Other	16 (2)	2

Previous clubs: Winchester City, Southampton

Many fans of Hereford United consider the capture of Terry Paine to be one of the most inspired signings ever made by the club. The former Southampton stalwart and England international joined Hereford United as a player, coach and captain with 19 full England caps to his name in July 1974. The former England and Southampton player was an all-time great at his former club. He made 713 appearances for the Saints, scoring 160 goals. Terry made his debut for Southampton in 1957 and only missed 28 League games out of a possible 820 in the next twenty years! He was a member of the 1966 World Cup-winning squad, arguably the greatest squad of players assembled by an England manager. He made one appearance for his country during the tournament in a 2-0 win against Mexico. When his international days ended he had scored 7 goals for England including a hat-trick against Northern Ireland in the first ever game to be played under floodlights at Wembley Stadium. The 8-3 rout in November 1963 saw Terry playing out on the right wing and his inside right partner was Jimmy Greaves, who scored four goals in that match. Terry's hat-trick was thought to be the first hat-trick scored by an England winger in a British Championship for seventy years. He signed for Hereford during the close season of 1974 and made 106 appearances, scoring 8 goals. Many Saints fans were disappointed when Terry left the club, and he would have stayed with them but he wanted to try football coaching. When his League debut for the club came on Saturday 17 August 1974 in a home fixture against Aldershot, some fans may have wondered if he still had the desire to play competitive football. They soon found out. Manager John Sillett blooded a number of new players that day but it was Terry Paine, with his vision and ball control, that caught the eye of many. The game ended in a 2-0 victory for the club, Terry setting up the second goal with a defence-splitting pass. John Sillett was quoted as saying, 'Signing Terry Paine for Hereford United was one hell of a good move for us.' Making 40 League appearances for the club during his first season he scored 4 goals. A number of player changes occurred for the beginning of the 1975/76 season in which the club finished up as Third Division champions. Again Terry Paine proved an inspiration and missed only a handful of games. Large crowds watched the team as they won the championship in convincing style. In October 1975 Terry made his record-breaking 765th League appearance against Peterborough United at Edgar Street, beating the record previously held by Jimmy Dickinson (Portsmouth) of 764 appearances by his fortieth birthday in 1965. Terry was only thirty-six when he achieved this.

Proving to be an inspiration to everyone, his enthusiasm on the pitch was infectious to players and fans alike. He was constantly demanding the ball as he organised the Hereford players around him, inspiring them to chase balls they felt they had no chance of getting. His knowledge and ability to read the game proved invaluable as another promotion season beckoned.

The following season, which proved to be the only one in the Second Division, Terry Paine surprised many when he announced his retirement after the away fixture against his former club Southampton on 16 October 1976. The game had ended in a 1-0 defeat for Hereford. However, only three games later after a change of heart, Terry Paine returned to the Hereford side in a home fixture against the League leaders Chelsea. The fixture, played on Saturday 6 November 1976, ended in a 2-2 draw in an exciting game before a crowd of 12,528. The season ended with Hereford being relegated and Terry Paine finally retiring. He had made 26 League appearances and scored 3 goals. Sadly his contribution was not enough to save the club from relegation.

Terry Paine broke the record for the highest number of Football League appearances while at Edgar Street and eventually gave up playing football after a total of 824 games. Phil Godsall of the supporters' club had this to say about Terry: 'Terry has graced the game with distinction and is undoubtedly the complete master of his craft, having given enjoyment to millions over the last eighteen years. I don't think any youngster wishing to take up the game could find a better example to follow than Terry, whose skill and ability to read the game is still up to First Division standard.' Frank Miles, chairman of Hereford United in 1975, also played tribute to Terry: 'Terry bubbles with enthusiasm and has become totally involved in the running of the club since he arrived. He sets a wonderful example to youngsters and also to the experienced playing staff. Terry Paine is a footballer extraordinaire, a man of unusual distinction'.

He later played for Cheltenham Town and had a spell coaching in South Africa. Then, in 1989, he teamed up again with John Sillett at Coventry City as reserve team coach.

Paine has scored for Hereford.

Paul Parry

Winger, 1998–2004

Conference era

	Appearances	Goals
League	136 (4)	29
Other	14	3

Previous clubs: Bristol City

Paul Parry is a winger of the highest calibre, who went on to gain his first full international cap for Wales within months of leaving Edgar Street. He can play a striker's role but prefers playing out on the wing, and he is happiest when he is setting up goals.

Paul was born in Newport, South Wales, on 19 August 1980. A natural left-footed midfield player, he was let go by Bristol City at the age of sixteen and signed YTS forms for Hereford United in 1997/98, United's debut campaign in the Conference. His first appearance for the Bulls was as a substitute in the away match at Dover Athletic in March 1998, United gaining a 1-1 draw. He signed professional forms in 1998 and played his first game as a professional in 1998/99, coming on as a substitute in the 3-2 defeat away at Leek Town in November. Paul started to stake a claim for a regular first-team place, scoring against Kidderminster Harriers at Aggborough in the Conference Trophy. Unfortunately, his first few seasons at Edgar Street were dogged by injury and illness. At the start of the 1999/2000 season he was diagnosed with glandular fever and it took him a year to get over it, Paul had to work hard to regain his fitness. However, he recovered to win back his place in the team just before the Bulls' FA Cup run, which culminated in matches home and away against Leicester City. He played brilliantly in the matches against the Foxes; the press reviews raved about Paul and he gained the interest of many Football League scouts. He hit the post in the first match at Edgar Street with Tim Flowers, the former England goalkeeper, in goal for Leicester. If that goal had gone in it would have come close to being as famous as Ron Radford's goal against Newcastle. A lot of the 2000/01 season was spent on the sidelines as Paul ruptured his ankle ligaments. It was some time before the full extent of his injury was known, delaying his return to fitness. Paul was selected to play in the Unibond Four Nations Tournament in 2002 and helped Wales to win it, playing against teams from England, Scotland and Ireland. It was a very interesting tournament as Hereford United had players in the England squad – Matt Baker and Michael Rose – with Tony James also chosen for the Welsh squad. It certainly made for interesting banter in the dressing room prior to the tournament!

Paul Parry

Winger, 1998–2004

Paul Parry on the wing for Hereford, *c.* 2001.

In an amazing 7-1 win away at Forest Green Rovers Paul scored his only hat-trick for Hereford United. Paul played his last game for the Bulls at Edgar Street on 3 January 2004, against Stevenage, scoring the only goal of the game in injury time. Although many clubs, including Glasgow Celtic (managed by Martin O'Neill, ex-manager of Leicester City), were rumoured to be interested in Paul Parry he was finally signed by Cardiff City in January 2004 and within months gained a full international cap for Wales. The fee was an initial £75,000, but increased to £200,000 based on first-team appearances and winning an international cap. He made his debut for Cardiff on 10 January against Rotherham, the Bluebirds winning 3-2. On 18 February Paul made his debut for Wales, playing against Scotland in a friendly. He came on in the thirty-third minute replacing Simon Davies, who was a Tottenham Hotspur player at the time. He made an immediate impact, winning the ball and passing it to Ryan Giggs, who crossed the ball for Earnshaw to put it in the back of the net. He made his first start for Wales in Norway in May 2004, taking the number eleven shirt from Ryan Giggs who was injured, and played the whole of the ninety minutes. On 30 May 2004 Paul scored his first goal for Wales in a friendly at home to Canada, in a match played on Wrexham's ground. It was the only goal of the game and, unusually for Paul, it was a header! This was followed in September 2004 by his first competitive debut for Wales, coming on as a substitute against Northern Ireland in a World Cup qualifier.

Paul made a total of 154 appearances for Hereford United, scoring 32 goals. He is a truly exceptional winger who can operate on either flank. He is a natural left-footer and thus prefers to play on the left, but has the ability to cut inside defenders when playing on the right wing. The Edgar Street faithful were disappointed to see Paul Parry leave, but all wished him great success, a name to look out for in the future.

Darren Peacock

Midfield, 1989–1990

Football League era

	Appearances	Goals
League	56 (3)	4
Other	12	1

Previous clubs: Newport County

Darren Peacock arrived at Edgar Street from a football club that had just folded and was to be a saviour for Hereford United when his transfer fee helped to prevent the Bulls from going the same way. He was born in Bristol on 3 February 1968 and he joined Newport County as an apprentice when the Welsh side were managed by Colin Addison. He made an immediate impact in Newport's youth side, scoring 5 goals in his first 2 games in the Gwent Sunday Youth League. He made his Football League debut at the age of seventeen as a substitute against Plymouth in 1985, and a couple of weeks later Darren was in the starting line-up against Walsall. He made a total of 18 appearances for Newport in his first season. Among his teammates was Richard Jones (who went on to play for United and was voted Player of the Year in 1989), who described Darren as having very short hair in those days – different to his time at Edgar Street where he was renowned for his long wavy hair! Darren made a total of 28 Football League appearances for Newport and played regularly for them in the GM Vauxhall Conference after they had been relegated. However, the professional career of Darren looked doomed in February 1989 when Newport County finally folded after half a season in the Conference. The club had been struggling financially for a number of years. They were dark and dismal days for the youngster; he remembers not knowing when he might get paid. The club managed on a day-to-day existence and when they finally packed up the players were left to search for new clubs. They were free to join whoever they chose.

Ian Bowyer, who was manager of Hereford United, spotted the potential in Darren and brought him to Edgar Street. He made his debut for Hereford United as a substitute at Colchester in April 1989 and his full debut at Grimsby two weeks later. Darren played 8 times in the Bulls' first team that season. He played mainly in defence but he was versatile enough to play a few games in attack when needed.

The following season saw Darren turn in some very solid performances, which endeared him to the fans. He scored twice in the opening game of the season against Swindon Town in the Herefordshire Senior Cup final and scored his first Football League goal for United against Carlisle United. He was always very reliable and gave 100 per cent on the pitch. His consistency and commitment over the season led to him being voted Player of the Year. Despite his six feet two inches height and his no-nonsense approach on the football pitch, as Bulls captain Darren was a very shy person off the pitch. During his first season with United he refused to fill in a player profile form because he did not think that anyone would be interested in his likes and dislikes!

One of the most important games of Darren's career while playing for Hereford United was the Welsh FA Cup final against Wrexham in May 1990. Darren had to pass a fitness test on the morning of the match. Others, such as Ian Juryeff, were not so lucky. United went ahead in the thirty-fourth minute when Gary Bowyer took a free-kick on the right-hand side of the area. His perfect cross was met by Darren, who knocked the ball down for Colin Robinson to put in the back of the net. Wrexham equalised through Gary Worthington but United were not to be denied victory, Ian Benbow scoring the winner.

Darren's consistent performances were always going to attract the scouts of bigger clubs and it was no surprise when he was transferred to Queens Park Rangers just before the Christmas of 1990 for £200,000. This beat the previous club record when Phil Stant was transferred to Notts County. Darren was thrown straight into a struggling Rangers side, and admits that it took a while to settle in. 'The pace of the game was quicker, not physically but mentally. The game in the last third of the field is very fast,' was his comment. Darren soon got used to it, however, and formed a solid partnership with the Northern Ireland skipper Alan McDonald. His long dark hair and tough tackling made him a big favourite with the Queens Park Rangers fans. He showed that he was every bit as good if not better than the players of Leeds United and Manchester United, who Rangers beat by four goals, and that he could compete with the best in the country. He later moved to Newcastle United, who were under the management of Kevin Keegan, for a staggering £2.7 million fee in 1994. When United had allowed Darren to leave they had negotiated a sell-on clause, and so profited from the deal by some £245,000, funds that were greatly needed and appreciated by manager Greg Downs.

Darren Peacock with a young fan.

Mel Pejic

Midfield, 1980–1992

Football League era

	Appearances	Goals
League	404 (8)	14
Other	41 (3)	6

Previous clubs: Stoke City

Mel Pejic was arguably the most dependable, loyal and popular player ever to represent Hereford United Football Club. Mel, brother of former Stoke, Everton and England full-back Mike Pejic, joined the club from Stoke City in July 1980. His popularity has been underlined by the fact that he was the first player to have been voted Player of the Year by supporters on three successive occasions, and on his arrival at Edgar Street he proved to be a great ambassador for the club. During his twelve years at the club Mel made 413 League appearances and thus beat the highest aggregate record set by Chris Price.

Mel was born in Newcastle-under-Lyme on 27 April 1959 and, from the time he started to kick a tennis ball around as a small child, it seemed inevitable that he would become a professional football player. His brother Mike, who was nine years older than Mel, was beginning to emerge as a talented young player and it was not long before football became one of the main topics of conversation in the Pejic household. While his brother moved on to professional duties with Stoke City, Mel was making progress at school level as a promising young inside forward and was eventually selected to play for Newcastle-under-Lyme schoolboys and then the Staffordshire youth team.

Mel was invited as a young teenager to go down to the Victoria Ground on his school holidays to play in trial matches after Mike had become a first-team regular with Stoke City. Mel's hopes of following in his brother's footsteps as an apprentice with Stoke City were not realised and he then had trials with Wolves and Port Vale. But he always wanted to play for Stoke City and was eventually taken on by the club as a junior by George Eastham, who was manager at the time. On 12 January 1980 he made his first-team debut at the Victoria Ground in the number two shirt when Stoke City entertained Ipswich Town in the First Division. He was not retained by Stoke City at the end of the season and was offered terms by Hereford United manager Frank Lord. Sadly, for both Hereford and Mel, he had an unfortunate start to this career with United, when he injured his knee in the third game of the season at Mansfield Town on 23 August 1980, and had to undergo two operations. This kept him out of the game for six months, and the following season it happened again, in the first game of the new campaign against Sheffield United at

Mel Pejic

Midfield, 1980–1992

Bramall Lane. This time, happily, the damage to the torn ligaments was not quite as serious, and he recovered sufficiently to play in the last 27 League games of the season. This was enough to earn him a new contract and for the next four seasons he only missed 5 out of a possible 236 League and cup games. Mel's first goal for United came in the Milk Cup first round second leg at Edgar Street when the Bulls lost 1-2 to Cardiff City. He was rated one of the best defenders in the Fourth Division and was voted United's Player of the Year in 1983, 1984 and 1985. At only five feet seven inches Mel was not the customary central defender but few taller strikers were able to get the better of him. The Hereford United defence of Chris Price, Keith Hicks, Mel Pejic and Ian Bray were formidable and, during the 1984/85 season, were more or less ever present. United narrowly missed out on promotion after finishing fifth, seven points behind the fourth-placed club Bury.

One of his goals was scored against Portsmouth in the Milk Cup first round first leg at Edgar Street during the 1983/84 season. He scored the winner, smashing the ball into the back of the net after John Black had headed back across goal, United winning the match 3-2. However, Hereford United lost on aggregate 4-5. Mel retained many happy memories of his long spell at Edgar Street and rated the four cup matches with Arsenal among the highlights, especially the 1-1 draw in the first clash at Edgar Street. He scored a consolation goal for United at Highbury when Arsenal beat them 7-2, equalling United's heaviest defeat in this competition (Kidderminster Harriers having beaten them by the same scoreline in 1924). Memories of this defeat were mostly eradicated the following season when Hereford United drew the Gunners again, this time in the Milk Cup. The first leg at Edgar Street was goal-less but the second leg ended in victory for Arsenal by only one goal, the result being 2-1. Mel's biggest match was as captain against Manchester United in the FA Cup fourth-round tie on 28 January 1990, when the Bulls lost 1-0 to a late Clayton Blackmore goal in front of a crowd of 13,777. Mel had scored a dramatic last-gasp winner against Walsall in the third round to make sure of progressing to the next round, when a draw had looked inevitable. He also had his share of disappointments as a Hereford United player. These included the time when United lost 3-0 to Bristol City on 9 May

Pejic scores a rare goal in Hereford United colours.

1986 in the Freight Rover Trophy semi-final, after winning the first leg 2-0, and missed out on a trip to Wembley. Another major disappointment was the end-of-season collapse when the team looked certain to win promotion to the Third Division at the end of the 1984/85 season.

Mel played in many exciting and entertaining games while with Hereford United. Perhaps one of the most exciting occurred on Wednesday 6 March 1985 when Hereford beat Bury in a vital 5-3 win at Edgar Street before a crowd of 4,600. After the win many fans felt that promotion was a certainty but this, sadly, was not the case. Perhaps his greatest day as a Hereford United player was on 13 May 1990 when Mel Pejic captained the Bulls as they won the Welsh Cup at Cardiff Arms Park with a 2-1 win over Wrexham. Hereford United had been entering the Welsh Cup since 1936 and, after a number of Welsh Cup final defeats, they at last won the competition after fifty-four years, becoming one of the few English clubs to take the cup out of Wales.

After the Welsh Cup final Ian Bowyer, manager of Hereford United, released Mel but he was quickly re-signed by United's new manager Colin Addison, who wasted no time in making him his first signing. Mel was ever present in the Bulls team in the 1990/91 season, his eleventh season with the club.

During his time with Hereford Mel scored around 20 goals for the club in all competitions. However, his outstanding ability at defending was a far more vital contribution to the team. He won the respect of all Hereford United fans, managers and teammates. One manager said of him, 'Our players like him, their players like him, our fans like him, their fans like him. I just wish occasionally somebody would hate him!' Mel Pejic later moved to Wrexham, where he again proved what an effectual defender he was.

Pejic poses for a publicity shot.

Striker, 1978–1988, 1990–1991

Football League era

	Appearances	Goals
League	316 (14)	95
Other	31 (2)	14

Previous clubs: West Browich Albion, Swansea City

Stewart Phillips was a fantastic centre forward and goal-scorer for Hereford United and, in his two stints with the Edgar Street club, reached many milestones. These included being the first player to score a hat-trick in an away match in the Football League. He also scored 100 goals for United, the first player since John Charles to reach that figure and the first Hereford United player to do so in the Football League era. He was born in Halifax in December 1961, but was brought up in Hereford, where he went to Haywood High School. It was while he was still at school, aged sixteen years and 112 days, that Stewart took an afternoon off to make his debut for United, in April 1978, away at Swindon Town. It was not the best of results for your debut match, United losing by the only goal of the game, but Hereford could take home a lot of pluses in a match that saw the Bulls field six players under twenty-one in their line-up. Seven months later Stewart signed full professional forms for Hereford United and made 5 appearances in a season that saw the Bulls finish fourteenth in the Fourth Division. The following season saw Stewart play in 10 League games and, more importantly, start his goal-scoring for United. The first goal came in a 2-1 home win against Wigan Athletic, Paul Hunt scoring the other goal. Stewart went on to be United's top scorer in four successive seasons, 1981/82 (16), 1982/83 (14), 1983/84 (19) and 1984/85 (22, the same as Ollie Kearns). Although he was not such a natural goal-scorer as Dixie McNeil, Charlie Thompson or John Charles, he was extremely consistent in his quality of play and the goals he scored. He was a great ambassador for the club over a number of seasons, and always deserved to be selected for the first team, although there were a few who thought it was more to do with the fact that his father was a director of the club. Stewart's first hat-trick came in a home match against Chester on 5 February 1983, Hereford United gaining revenge on a 5-0 defeat at Sealand Road earlier in the season. Stewart was the first player to score a hat-trick in the League since Dixie McNeil. The only other player to do so was Frank McGrellis. The win was even more remarkable as Chester took the lead, but the Bulls came back to score twice in sixty seconds. Teasdale scored the first goal after Chester's goalkeeper Harrington had parried a header from Stewart. A minute later Ian Bray sent over a cross and this time Harrington could not prevent Stewart from scoring. It was Danny Bartley who set up Stewart's other two goals. The 5-2 victory was a brilliant game in a season that had more downs than ups for United. There were three changes at management level and with a very small playing squad it was a very

difficult season. It ended with United finishing bottom of the League. The finances were so bad that a 'Save our Soccer' appeal was in operation to help stave off the threat of liquidation. Stewart only missed a handful of games the previous two seasons, but 1983/84 saw Stewart ever present, along with goalkeeper Kevin Rose, and the fans were given a boost with United finishing midway in the table. In 1984/85 Stewart was also given the accolade of being voted a member of the PFA Fourth Division XI by his fellow professionals, along with Jimmy Harvey and Chris Price. His goal-scoring abilities (the number of goals scored by Stewart each season was steadily increasing) were attracting the attention of many League clubs, including Manchester City. Unfortunately, Stewart's injury-free run came to an end and he was forced to sit out more than half of the following season. United enjoyed a magnificent run of victories at home but their away performances were dismal. The 1986/87 season saw Stewart obtain another club record by scoring the Bulls' first hat-trick in an away match in the Football League. Burnley were the team on the wrong end of a 6-0 defeat at Turf Moor while they were enduring a particularly bad spell at the wrong end of the Football League. Jimmy Harvey opened the scoring from the penalty spot after the Burnley goalkeeper had impeded Ian Wells. This was to be their goalkeeper's first and last appearance for Burnley! It was also the season that saw Stewart score his 100th goal for United, away at Northampton Town. Although United lost the match 3-2, a late strike from Stewart was ruled out by the referee. In 1988, after 293 appearances for Hereford United in the Football League and scoring 83 goals, Stewart was transferred to West Bromwich Albion. The assistant manager at The Hawthorns was none other than Colin Addison. West Bromwich were struggling to avoid relegation from the Second Division, and this was achieved with the help of Stewart. He went on to play for Swansea City before returning to Edgar Street at the start of the 1990/91 season, first of all on loan, but with the move then being made permanent (bringing Stewart back under the management of Colin Addison). His first two appearances in his second spell for United were as a substitute but he reopened his goal-scoring in a Bulls shirt at home to York City. A major milestone was reached when Stewart played his 300th League game for United at home to Stockport County on 29 September 1990. He was only the third player to do so, joining the exclusive club formed by Mel Pejic and Chris Price. The match was a very scrappy goal-less draw and Stewart was guilty of missing some very good chances. A few weeks later Stewart returned to his home town of Halifax and scored another hat-trick away from home (the only player to achieve this feat for United), with on-loan striker Paul Millar scoring the other in a 4-0 victory. By the end of the season Stewart had scored 93 goals, beating the record set by Dixie McNeil. He made 31 appearances that season although his goal-scoring was not so prolific, registering only 11 goals. However, the highest goal-scorer for the Bulls was Jon Narbett, and he only managed 12, and this was still an improvement on the previous season when the top scorer was Mark Jones with 9 goals.

Stewart's last game for Hereford United was away at Peterborough United in May 1991, at the end of a very illustrious career in football. He had a remarkable knack for scoring goals in both the League and in cup runs and he remains very popular with the fans. He has opened up a fitness suite in Hereford and can very often be seen up in the stand at Edgar Street, watching his old club. He is a keen follower of the sport and is ever ready to help out in any fundraising events, a credit to the sport we all love so much.

Winston White looks on as Phillips scores.

Phillips heads for goal, *c.* 1985.

Jamie Pitman

Midfield, 1995–1998, 2002–

Football League era

	Appearances	Goals
League	16 (5)	
Other	3 (1)	

Conference era

	Appearances	Goals
League	156 (7)	10
Other	11	7

Previous clubs: Southampton, Swindon Town, Yeovil Town, Woking

Jamie Pitman is a gutsy midfield player who, although lacking in height, and having suffered some major injuries, makes determined performances on the pitch of a consistently high standard. He is a grafter who never gives up running and all the fans can see how much he enjoys his chosen sport.

Jamie was born in Trowbridge, Wiltshire, on 6 January 1976, and started his career at the age of ten years at Southampton Football Club, before being released at the age of sixteen. After going to trials at a number of football clubs Jamie was taken on as an apprentice at Swindon Town for two years in June 1992. Here Jamie was quick to learn his trade with a team that finished runners-up in the South-East Counties League, the first team being managed by none other than Glenn Hoddle, who was, Jamie admits, his childhood hero. In the first season that Jamie was there Swindon won promotion to the Premier League, but unfortunately relegation quickly followed. He signed his first professional contract at Swindon in the 1994/95 season and made his first-team debut as a substitute against Notts County. After making 5 appearances Jamie signed for another season but in February Steve McMahon, who was manager by then at the County Ground, released Jamie and he came to Edgar Street. Here he obtained valuable first-team experience as a wing-back. Hereford United were enjoying a good spell in Division Three and eventually made it into the play-offs where they met Darlington. The Quakers proved to be United's bogey team; they had beaten United by the only goal of the game twice in the League and in the play-offs they again won both matches 2-1. The following season saw the start of Jamie's injury woes as he dislocated his shoulder and was forced to miss most of the season, which was to end in United's relegation from the Football League after twenty-five years, a day that Jamie describes as the worst of his life.

Now in the Football Conference, Jamie made 30 appearances for Hereford United before joining fellow Conference rivals Yeovil Town for the 1998/99 season. It was at this point that Jamie decided to go part-time and obtain an education at college. Unfortunately more ill luck followed as Jamie broke his leg twice, but he regained his fitness and was a regular member of the Huish Park first team the following season. He moved to another Conference side when he joined Woking for the 2000/01 season, who were under the management of Colin Lippiatt, the manager who had taken Jamie to Yeovil. By this time Jamie had moved back to Hereford to live, and was working part-time for the Hereford Leisure Centre. The travelling backwards and forwards to Woking for training and playing in matches proved to be too much and he returned to play at Edgar Street in 2002. Although still troubled by injuries, Jamie shows great determination to get back into the first team and finds being injured very frustrating. He is a great ambassador for the sport he clearly enjoys and a fantastic team player. He loves the lifestyle that the sport has brought him and enjoys the time off he gets, although he has to juggle the sport with his job as a fitness instructor. However, he rarely misses a training session for the Bulls. He admits to hating losing matches and to knowing that his football career cannot last forever. Two of his lowest moments in the sport were losing in the play-offs of the Conference; he says 'if you finish second over forty-two games you are the second best in the League and deserve to be promoted.' The Hereford United team of 2003/04 was the best group of players he has ever been with, their team spirit plain to see on and off the pitch. Jamie loves the competitive aspect of the game, saying 'you can't beat trying to be better than your opponents.' He is very lucky to be doing a job that he clearly enjoys, and loves scoring goals, although admits it does not happen as often as he would like: 'You really enjoy playing in the big games when the pressure is on and you are really nervous.' During his time at Edgar Street Jamie has seen some of the ups and most of Hereford United's downs, but has found it to be most enjoyable. 'The great FA Cup runs, the two seasons finishing runners-up in the Conference and being a member of the great 2003/04 team who unfortunately missed out on automatic promotion by one point to Chester City were brilliant. The club has got better and better over the last few seasons and will continue to progress and I would love to still be a part of that progress.'

Pitman scores for Hereford.

Fred Potter

Goalkeeper, 1970–1974

Prior to 1972/73

	Appearances	Clean sheets
	122	58

Football League era

	Appearances	Clean sheets
League	10	4
Other	1	

Previous clubs: Aston Villa, Doncaster Rovers, Burton Albion

Fred Potter started his footballing career as an inside forward but successfully converted to a goalkeeper who was an integral member of the Hereford United 'Giant-killing' team. He had a fantastic record of keeping clean sheets and had the honour of playing for Aston Villa and Doncaster Rovers before finding his niche in non-League football.

Fred was born in Cradley Heath in November 1940 and played for the junior teams of Aston Villa as an inside forward before changing to play in goal for them, thus initiating a career that would see Fred taking on the likes of England's Geoff Hurst. Fred signed as a full professional at Villa Park in July 1959 at the age of eighteen and he made his debut for Aston Villa against Wolverhampton Wanderers on Boxing Day 1960. However, the chances of first-team appearances with the Midlands club were limited and Fred decided to make the move to Belle Vue, home of Doncaster Rovers, in July 1962. Here he quickly established himself as the natural first-team choice for Rovers and, over the next three seasons, he was virtually an ever-present in the side. When an injury crisis struck the club, Fred even reverted back to making an appearance as an outfield player, such was his versatility!

Fred made a total of 123 League appearances before making the move into non-League football, linking up with Burton Albion. Here he quickly earned the reputation of being one of the most difficult goalkeepers to beat at this level of football. His succession of spectacular performances earned him the Player of the Year trophy from the Brewers fans at Eton Park, showing how popular he had made himself with them.

John Charles noted how good Fred was in goal and was quick to persuade him to come to Edgar Street and join the Bulls in September 1970. He made his debut for Hereford United on 26 September 1970 in an away match at Bedford Town, and the following week, on 3 October, Fred made his debut at Edgar Street in a sound 4-0 win against visiting Poole Town. This win was United's sixth successive home victory and took the club to the top of the Southern League Premier Division. Out of 60 first-team appearances that season, Fred kept 20 more clean sheets. He was a member of the team that beat Northampton Town of the Football League in a

Fred Potter with the Player of the Year trophy at the end of the marvellous 1971/72 season.

second-round replay at the County Ground, to make sure of a third-round tie against Brighton. They also came within ninety minutes of playing at Wembley but lost in the semi-final of the FA Trophy to Hillingdon Borough.

The following season saw an even more impressive display as Fred played in 61 first-team fixtures, keeping clean sheets in 38 of those matches. The matches included friendlies against League opposition in Walsall and Mansfield Town and, of course, the goal-less FA Cup matches against Northampton Town and West Ham United. Fred certainly played his part in making sure that the team of 1971/72 will be forever written into the history books of Hereford United. Even England international

Fred Potter

Goalkeeper, 1970–1974

Geoff Hurst, Clyde Best, Harry Redknapp, Trevor Brooking and Bryan Robson could not get past our Fred in goal on 9 February 1972. His outstanding performances between the goal-posts during the whole of the season made him an instant hit with the fans at Edgar Street, and they duly rewarded him with the Player of the Year trophy at the end of the 1971/72 season. The following season saw Fred Potter line up in goal in Hereford United's debut in the Football League on 12 August 1972, following their election at the expense of Barrow, United gaining twenty-nine votes in the final ballot against Barrow's twenty. He played in their first eight matches, keeping three clean sheets against Reading, Workington and Gillingham before losing his place to David Icke, who had been signed from Coventry City. Following Icke's retirement from football at the end of the season, due to severe arthritis, Fred made a comeback to first-team football, but he suffered a broken wrist on the opening day of the 1973/74 season away at Grimsby Town in the eighty-seventh minute. He had given another brilliant display in goal, including a superb first-half penalty save. This match turned out to be his last game for Hereford United, which was very sad as he had been a marvellous asset for the club. Out of 131 matches Fred had kept a total of 62 clean sheets – what a record! He has been described as unflappably phlegmatic, a real Brummie and quite a character, who will always retain a place in the hearts of the older generation of Hereford United fans.

Chris Price

Defender, 1978–1986

Football League era

	Appearances	Goals
League	327 (3)	26
Other	36	2

Chris Price had the enviable distinction of becoming Hereford United's youngest player, at the age of twenty years and seven months, to make his 100th Football League appearance, in a match played at Halifax in a Fourth Division fixture in October 1980. A local lad, Chris was born in Hereford in March 1960. After playing local football he was signed as an associated schoolboy in November 1974 and signed apprentice forms in June 1976. He was selected to play for the English national team at youth level, playing against Norway at Craven Cottage, home of Fulham Football Club. A couple of days after his seventeenth birthday Chris make his debut in a Second Division match against Notts County and signed a full-time contract in January 1978. Chris was only the tenth player to top 100 League appearances for United since they had been elected. From 1979 to 1986 he made the number two shirt his own and he became very popular with the Edgar Street fans because of his overlapping runs, which led him to scoring several goals and also winning the team a large number of penalties. His first goal did not come until the 1980/81 season. He scored against Rochdale in a Fourth Division match at Edgar Street, which United went on to win 2-0. Ten days later Chris was on the scoresheet again; this time Northampton Town were on the receiving end of a 4-1 victory.

He was very popular with his teammates and other Fourth Division teams rated him very highly, as the fact that he was regularly selected as a member of the PFA's Fourth Division XI showed. He was also voted Player of the Year at Hereford in 1981/82 and 1985/86. At the end of the 1981/82 season Chris Price was United's second-top scorer, having scored 10 goals. Probably Chris's most famous goal was scored against Arsenal in the FA Cup third-round tie at Edgar Street in January 1985. On a very cold day on a tricky, frozen pitch, United came close to causing a major upset. Tony Woodcock had put the Gunners ahead but twelve minutes later Chris struck the ball into the back of the net. United had the chances to go on and win the match and only some very brave goalkeeping kept Arsenal in the cup tie. Chris's equaliser earned United a lucrative replay at Highbury where unfortunately they were comprehensively beaten 7-2. Highbury was the location of another milestone in Chris Price's career the following season, when he made his 350th competitive first-team appearance in United's colours. This time United only lost by a single goal. Four days later Chris made his 300th Football League appearance for United at home to Torquay United in October 1985, and the Bulls made it a day to remember by winning 4-1. Chris was still aged only twenty-five. News of his great ability on the football pitch spread to other Football League clubs. His surging runs at defenders made at every opportunity, his consistency and his extrovert personality brought him to the attention of the League scouts as well as the United fans. After playing in a Hereford United shirt for ten years and being the first-choice right-back for seven seasons, Chris was given the chance to prove himself on a bigger stage. Blackburn Rovers were the club to put in an offer for him in 1986, although it was for a derisory £25,000 fee. He spent two seasons at Ewood Park, during which Blackburn featured prominently in the promotion race, but on both occasions narrowly missed promotion to the First Division. Chris made 83 League appearances for them, and also played in the Full Members Cup final at Wembley. Two years after moving to Blackburn he attracted the attention of Graham Taylor, who paid £150,000 to take him to Villa Park. This move also boosted United's bank balance by £12,500, agreed as part of the package deal when Chris moved to Blackburn. He was a regular in the Aston Villa team, playing in Europe in the UEFA Cup. Despite his fame and popularity Chris remained level headed and unassuming, a credit to his profession. He returned to Blackburn Rovers for a while before joining Portsmouth. When talking of players who have worn a Hereford United shirt, the Bulls fans will always bring up the name of Chris Price. He was an important member of the team for many seasons and thoroughly deserved his popularity. His enthusiasm for the sport and the qualities he brought to the club will long be remembered.

Price in action.

Ron Radford

Midfield, 1971–1974

Prior to 1972/73

	Appearances	Goals
	64	

Football League era

	Appearances	Goals
League	61	6
Other	8	

Previous clubs: Sheffield United, Leeds United, Cheltenham Town, Newport County

Ron Radford was born in South Elmshall in South Yorkshire in July 1943 and signed amateur forms for Sheffield Wednesday in the 1959/60 season before joining Leeds United as a professional in October 1961. It proved to be difficult to break into the first team at Elland Road and Ron moved to Cheltenham, where he established his own carpentry and joinery business. He joined Cheltenham Town as a part-timer, playing regularly for the Robins in the Southern League for six years. In July 1969 he moved to Somerton Park and was a regular with Newport County, playing in the Football League, making his League debut at the age of twenty-six. Ron Radford was a right-sided midfielder and scored 7 goals in 63 appearances over two seasons for Newport. John Charles, the Bulls' manager, had watched some of the mid-week matches at Newport and he persuaded Ron to join Hereford United for £1,000 in July 1971. This enabled Ron to continue with his carpentry business and play football on a part-time basis. He became a regular choice in the starting line-up at Edgar Street and his long-range shooting ability was prominent in the Southern League Premier Division before it took the country by storm. He was once described by a fellow teammate as a midfield player with talent, commitment and a warm and generous nature whom everyone loved. He was a very quiet man but always smiling, and he had a very modest nature. He is best known for his memorable goal against Newcastle United at Edgar Street, one of the most famous goals ever scored in the FA Cup and one which is still featured on television over thirty years on whenever the FA Cup matches come around. In the eighty-second minute, and against the run of play, Viv Busby had crossed the ball into the penalty area and Malcolm Macdonald had deflected it past Hereford United's goalkeeper Fred Potter to put Newcastle United one goal in front. United, however, refused to give up and kept pressing forward to get an equaliser, despite John Motson, the rookie BBC commentator saying 'That's it.'

The ball was won by substitute Ricky George, chasing back on the left-hand side of the pitch, with eighty-seven minutes on the clock. He slipped it inside to Ken Mallender, who knocked it into midfield. Ron Radford challenged for the

Ron Radford

Midfield, 1971–1974

ball with John Tudor of Newcastle, winning it at the second attempt, and passed it forward to Brian Owen, who played it back to Radford, who had not stopped running. At least thirty yards from goal Radford shot with his right foot and put the ball into the top right-hand corner of McFaul's goal. Newcastle United's and Northern Ireland's goalkeeper got nowhere near the ball. This goal became Goal of the Season in 1971/72 and remains one of the most featured goals on television. He is quoted as saying, 'You don't think about it, nor look up to place it. If it's 'on' and you can see the white sticks, have a go.' In extra time it was Ron Radford's turn to become the provider. He passed the ball six yards to Dudley Tyler, who then passed to ball to Ricky George to control at the second attempt and fire the winner past McFaul. Thousands of Hereford United fans invaded the football pitch at the end of the game to applaud their heroes, but Ron Radford escaped into the tunnel and had been in the players' bath before the others reached the changing room. He happily posed for photographers with the other players though, and there were some great shots taken of the two goal scorers. Hereford United presented Ron Radford with a rose bowl in recognition of his achievements and it took pride of place in his living room for many years. Ron Radford continued to help United as they won promotion from the Fourth Division in the club's first season in the Football League. He scored another spectacular goal at home to Northampton Town in the twelfth minute in a 2-0 victory. It was a left-foot drive from the edge of the box, his first League goal. He also scored two weeks

Ron Radford

Midfield, 1971–1974

Radford in action, 1972 – West Ham can only hope another thirty-five-yard goal will not happen.

running in March 1973, away to Northampton Town in a 4-0 victory (Eric Redrobe scored two and Billy Tucker the other) and at home to Peterborough United, when United won 3-0 (Owen and Jenkins were the other goal-scorers). Ron was a regular in the Hereford United Third Division side in 1973/74. Although most of his goals were long-range efforts from the edge of the penalty area, Ron Radford did score from a picture header against Wrexham in a 2-0 home win. Eric Redrobe was the other goal-scorer, although he had missed a penalty earlier in the match. This was Ron's first goal in the 1973/74 season. Hereford United supporters had to wait until February 1974 for another 'Radford special'. He scored from a superb twenty-five-yard drive in a match against Port Vale in a 2-1 win, Brian Owen scoring the other goal. A week later he scored another thirty-five-yard drive at Bournemouth but United lost 3-2 despite a goal from Tommy Naylor. In two seasons in the Football League Ron Radford made 61 appearances, scoring 6 goals. He also played in both the FA Cup matches against West Ham United in the 1973/74 season, although he picked up an injury in the first match at Upton Park. Ron Radford put in another thirty-yard shot in the replay at Edgar Street but this time the goalkeeper, Mervyn Day, was equal to it. Perhaps he had seen the video of the goal against Newcastle United! Hereford United still won the match 2-1 with goals from Tommy Naylor, a penalty, and Alan Jones. In a letter Ron described his days at Hereford as 'one big long happy memory. The spirit of the team, supporters and backroom staff was fantastic. The never-say-die fighting attitude of each and every player in the squad made it a time I will never forget and I consider myself very privileged to have been a part of it. We were all so very fortunate to have been in the right place at the right time. People ask me what I remember most about the time I had at Hereford and I can honestly say that it was not the goal that I scored, but it is the magnificent people that I came to know and love so dearly. I would not swap one moment of my time at Hereford United for all the money in the Premiership that is flowing at this moment in time, because what I have money cannot buy.' After leaving Hereford United Ron played for Worcester City before becoming manager of Ossett Albion, still maintaining a carpentry business in Leeds.

Although Ron did not easily cope with fame he attended many of the functions arranged for the Giant-killers and enjoyed their many reunions. Even more recent Hereford United players have found it difficult to live up to expectations; every time United play in the FA Cup one name comes back to haunt them – Ronnie Radford. It also comes back to haunt the Newcastle players. Willie McFaul, their goalkeeper, remembers the goal only too well, his outstretched hand was so close, yet so far away from stopping the shot. 'It was the worst pitch I played on in my life. We had plenty of opportunities to score goals but did not take them,' he said. 'The match had been off twice. We went into the game not as prepared as we should have been. Ronnie's goal was so special. I don't remember much about it, apart from Frank Clarke looking around at me in amazement. The ball seemed to sit up for Ronnie and he hit it. Every time I see it, I'm getting that little bit closer.'

A quote from the Sunday People stated, 'All hail to Hereford's lionhearted conquering heroes. The posters on the ground shouted "League status is our aim". You could have fooled me. I thought Hereford were after Wembley. So did Newcastle.' 'This incredible crazy combat of fury and passion stands alongside the greatest epics produced in FA Cup history and the happy farmers of Hereford became a singing chanting herd as highly charged as any who ever stood on the Liverpool Kop,' wrote the Sunday Express reporter. Yet for all the glory his goal brought, Ron prefers to talk about the wonderful team spirit in the club, and the incredible fans. 'Playing football is not just about the game, but it's more about the team spirit and the will to do your part in that team, if it's to be successful. To share the ups and to share the downs, to give that lift to others when they are down, and to be lifted by others when you, yourself, need a lift, it's a wonderful sharing experience that you never forget. Our games against Newcastle and West Ham will always be remembered with great affection and they did wonders for the county of Herefordshire.'

Eric Redrobe

Striker, 1972–1976

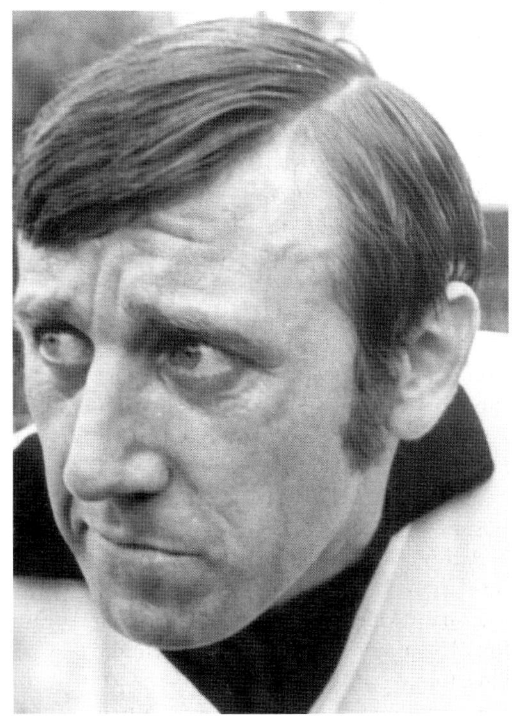

Football League era

	Appearances	Goals
League	75 (11)	18
Other	9 (2)	1

Previous clubs: Bolton Wanderers, Colchester United, Southport

A series of poor results saw Hereford United dropping into the re-election zone during their first season in the Football League in the 1972/73 season and something had to be done. Colin Addison, the Hereford United manager, acquired a striker who became a legend among the fans for his own particular style of football. Eric Redrobe was a fearsome figure with a wicked toothless grin who loved nothing better than trying to soften up the opposing goalkeeper. Without doubt the immediate impact he made at Edgar Street upon his arrival saw the team, who had won just twice in the opening fourteen games, begin a remarkable run that saw them climb up the table to second position in the division behind the champions-elect Southport.

Eric Redrobe was born in Wigan in August 1944 and was such a good overall sportsman that he was invited to play both football and rugby League for his home town. It was football that won over rugby, though, and then Eric chose Bolton Wanderers over his local side Wigan Athletic, signing junior forms for them. He worked his way up through the ranks before becoming a full-time professional in February 1962 at Burnden Park, after having had the honour of being selected to play for the England youth team. Eric scored his first League goal for Bolton in the 1963/64 season when he made 4 appearances for Bolton Wanderers in the Second Division. He signed for Colchester United in July 1966 but only stayed there a month before moving back up north, transferring to Southport, who were a Football League side at that time. He made his debut on 20 August 1966 against Port Vale, and he soon became a favourite with the home crowd at Haigh Avenue. His style of play, with body-checks and shoulder-charges, earned him the nickname of 'Big Red'. He scored their first goal in a 3-3 draw against Swindon Town in 1967/68 in a match that was featured on the BBC's *Match of the Day*, from twenty-five yards out. He was a strong, powerful player who used his six foot-plus frame to his best advantage.

Eric was top scorer for Southport in 1970/71 and again in 1971/72, in all scoring 55 goals in 192 League appearances for Southport. Colin Addison signed Eric Redrobe for Hereford United in 1972/73 for £6,000, in what was

Eric Redrobe

Striker, 1972–1976

Eric Redrobe in action.

seen to be a major coup for the Edgar Street manager. Eric had already made 9 appearances for Southport that season, including playing against Walsall in a League Cup match, during which Eric scored twice. He soon became a favourite at Edgar Street, scoring 18 goals in 87 appearances for Hereford United. His positive attitude helped transform the attacking options in United's first season in the Football League. The fans called Eric Redrobe 'The King of Edgar Street'. During this time United won promotion to the Third Division as runners-up behind Southport. The highlight of Eric Redrobe's career was the goal that he scored at Upton Park against West Ham on 5 January 1974 in front of a crowd of 23,087. This was a third-round FA Cup match and, when Eric Redrobe scored his goal in the twenty-third minute, it put Hereford United 1-0 up before substitute Pat Holland scored his late equaliser. When the final whistle blew at Upton Park Eric was the one player who did not know the score, having limped off the pitch with a knee injury early in the second half. He was so keyed up he waited in the dressing room with cotton wool in his ears! When the team returned to the dressing room, Eric thought United had lost the match, such was the disappointment of the equaliser. For the return match at Edgar Street a crowd of 17,423 and thousands more via *Match of the Day* saw Hereford United beat West Ham 2-1 in a fantastic match on a Wednesday afternoon. The country was in the middle of an industrial dispute and a three-day week and the government had banned the use of floodlights, but Hereford United were giant-killers yet again. There were Hereford United supporters on the roofs of nearby buildings and up in the surrounding trees, anywhere just to see the match.

Eric was also in the team that lifted the Third Division championship, having made 20 appearances for them in that season, scoring 1 goal, before being released in 1976. He had scored 18 League goals in 87 Football League appearances. He continued to play football for Bath City, Bridgend Town and Ledbury Town before returning to Edgar Street in 1978 as a non-contract player when Hereford had an injury crisis, but only made 1 appearance as a substitute. Since then Eric has played non-League football for Westfields and Presteigne St Andrews and rugby for Orrel Fourth XV, before moving back to Wigan to become a bailiff for the Lord Chancellor's Department. Eric still kept himself extremely fit and was even playing club rugby at the age of fifty-two.

Steve Ritchie

Defender, 1975–1978

Football League era

	Appearances	Goals
League	111 (2)	4
Other	15 (1)	2

Previous clubs: Bristol City, Greenock Morton

Steve Ritchie was a stylish, creative, attacking full-back who scored some powerful long-range goals. He played for a number of clubs, from Greenock Morton in Scotland to Torquay United in the South of England. He was born in Bo'ness, West Lothian, in February 1954, and was soon recognised as a footballer in the making when selected to play for Scotland at schoolboy level. He was signed up by Bristol City as an apprentice, linking up with his elder brother Tom Ritchie, who was already at Ashton Gate. Steve became a full professional in September 1971 but only played in one League game, before moving to the Scottish League side Greenock Morton. He was valued at £15,000 in a player exchange deal that saw Greenock's Don Gillies moving the other way to Ashton Gate. Steve made 65 League appearances for Morton and scored 1 goal, before being released in May 1975. John Sillett was manager of Hereford United at the time and he brought Steve to Edgar Street, the two linking up together for the second time as Sillett had been the football coach at Bristol City. Steve travelled to Holland with the Hereford United youth team who won the Blauw Wit Youth Tournament in the summer of 1975. He made his Third Division debut for the Bulls against Port Vale at Edgar Street in August 1975 and instantly became the first-choice left-back, making the number three shirt his. He was a popular player with the fans and players alike. When Hereford United won the Third Division championship, Steve Ritchie was the only player to have played in every single League match, forty-six games in all. John Sillett said at that time, 'Steve added steel to the defence where he is a natural left-sided player.' Even though he was a key defender, he also scored some very good goals. His first League goal for United was against Mansfield Town at Edgar Street, when he sent a lethal shot into the net from twenty-five yards. The away goalie, Arnold, got a hand to it but could not stop it. His other goal that season was in a magnificent 2-0 victory over Port Vale in the League Cup. The first-leg tie was played away from home and within forty-three minutes United were 4-0 down but staged an almighty comeback. With two goals from Jimmy Lindsay, one of which was set up by Steve Ritchie, they halved the deficit. The magnificent victory at Edgar Street meant another match against Port Vale, the fourth, including a League match, in seventeen days, and this time Hereford United were the victors by virtue of the one goal scored by Terry Paine.

Steve played regularly in Hereford United's season in the Second Division, scoring 1 goal, which was in the 2-2 draw at home to Chelsea, John Layton netting the other. Back in the Third Division Steve linked up well with Steve Emery, John Layton and Julian Marshall to form a solid defence, none of them letting the team down. He made 24 appearances and scored another goal before moving back north of the border, after being signed by Alex Ferguson to play for Aberdeen, for a fee of £10,000. He played in 9 Scottish Premier League games that season and scored Aberdeen's goal in the Scottish Cup final at Hampden Park in May 1978, in front of a crowd of 61,563, who saw them lose to Glasgow Rangers 2-1. Rangers completed the treble that season, winning the Scottish League, League Cup and Scottish FA Cup. Steve had also played for Hereford United in the final of the Welsh Cup against Cardiff City, so he is one of only a few players to have played in cup finals in both Scotland and Wales. Steve had made one other Scottish FA Cup appearance for Aberdeen, against Partick Thistle in the semi-final and this was also played at Hampden Park.

Steve played in only one more match for the Dons before moving a long way south to join Torquay United, going from the then most northerly Scottish League club to the most southerly English League club but one, second only to Plymouth Argyle. He made 58 appearances for Torquay before moving to non-League football teams Yeovil Town and Trowbridge Town. It came as no surprise when Steve's coaching skills gained prominence, first in the West Country before being given a very warm welcome back at Edgar Street when he returned as youth development coach. He worked well with the YTS lads and one of their achievements was to reach the last sixteen of the FA Youth Cup before Steve left Edgar Street for the second time.

David Rudge

Midfield, 1972–1975

Football League era

	Appearances	Goals
League	75 (7)	8
Other	9	

Previous clubs: Aston Villa

Midfielder David Rudge signed for Hereford United for a then-club record £6,000 from Aston Villa soon after United's election to the Football League. He made his debut at Bradford City on 26 August 1972 in an away fixture, the match ending in a 1-1 draw. The Wolverhampton-born player came to prominence as a schoolboy player and was snapped up by Aston Villa as an apprentice. He signed a full professional contract in May 1965. Rudgie had made 55 appearances for the Villa and scored 10 goals, making his debut for them in 1966/67 season. He attracted the attention of many scouts, including those of the national side, and it was not long before he was selected for the England youth team. While with the Villa he had won Aston Villa's Terrace Supporters' Trophy in 1969 but this was followed by a bad period as he later broke his leg – a misfortune he suffered for a second time during the season prior to joining Hereford United. When David signed for Hereford United it came as quite a shock to some ofVilla's Holte End supporters. He joined at the same time as Harry Gregory and the pair had already built up quite an understanding at Villa Park. His vital League experience proved invaluable to Hereford as the club strove firstly for consolidation in the Football League and later for end-of-season glory and promotion. He soon became a popular figure with many of the fans as his hard-working style of play combined with energetic and sometimes strength-sapping runs provided many scoring chances for his teammates. David scored his first League goal for Hereford in a vital 1-0 home victory against fellow promotion contenders Aldershot on 25 November 1972, a victory that extended the club's unbeaten run to six matches at that time. Aldershot at that time were fourth in the League, while United were way behind in thirteenth but moving up the table rapidly. He scored direct from a corner less than a month later on a bitterly cold evening away at Stockport County to ensure that United came away with a point. In January David opened the scoring against Chester at Edgar Street in the tenth minute. Eric Redrobe then grabbed a brace to make sure of both points and put United into contention for promotion. In all Rudge made 31 League appearances for the club during the season, scoring 3 goals. Unfortunately, due to injury,

David Rudge missed the last eight games of the season and had to sit though the nail-biting matches against Crewe Alexandra and Newport County on the sidelines, just like the 12,000-plus crowds. During the 1973/74 season David made 27 appearances scoring 3 goals, including the eighty-seventh-minute winner against Blackburn Rovers on a bitterly cold afternoon on 1 January 1974 after being recalled to the team. No doubt the winner, scored from fifteen yards, was the icing on the cake to arguably one of his finest games in a Hereford United shirt. His efforts were well rewarded as he kept his place for the vital and prestigious away fixture the following Saturday against West Ham United in a third-round FA Cup tie. The return fixture, played the following Wednesday afternoon, was memorable for David as he became a Hereford United Giant-killer with the Bulls winning 2-1 in front of a large crowd and television cameras. In February 1974 Hereford United were playing away to Rochdale and David Rudge scored a great goal for United. Dudley Tyler crossed the ball over to Rudge on the outside of the box and he volleyed it into the goal, a great low shot into the far corner of the net to beat goalkeeper Poole. Unfortunately, United let the lead slip and Rochdale managed to equalise through Brennan. David was an excellent crosser of the ball and his corner kicks were extremely accurate with either foot. He was well known for his work-rate and attitude on the pitch. He was an honest player and was always there to help out in difficult situations. In all David made 100 appearances for Hereford United, the last of which was away at Shrewsbury Town on 27 December 1975 as a substitute. He later transferred to Torquay United where he continued his playing career, making 64 League appearances for the Gulls, before joining non-League Barnstaple Town, who played in the Western League. No doubt he retained fond memories of Hereford United and their fans after his playing career ended.

David Rudge celebrates a goal for Hereford.

Kevin Sheedy

Midfield, 1976–1978

Football League era

	Appearances	Goals
League	47 (4)	3
Other	4 (1)	1

Not many players have had the distinction of playing for both Liverpool and Everton in their career but former Hereford United favourite Kevin Sheedy is one of them. He was born in Builth Wells in Wales in October 1959, but he had an Irish father, so he was eligible to play for both Wales and Eire. He chose Eire and was selected for their youth team against West Germany in a friendly while at Edgar Street in 1977 youth, and later won caps for the full international team.

He joined Hereford United as an apprentice and made his Football League debut with them before signing as a professional in October 1976. In the same season that the first team won the Third Division, Hereford United's youth side also won the Midland Intermediate Youth League. In the youth side were Kevin Sheedy, Chris Price, Steve Emery, Brian Preece and Julian Marshall, who all went on to play in the Football League for the Bulls. Kevin Sheedy had made such a good impression playing as a left-sided midfielder for the youth team that he was given his chance in the final match of the season on 28 April 1976 against Preston North End at the young age of sixteen, making an impressive debut. There were wild scenes of celebration at the end of that game, which the Bulls won 3-1 with a hat-trick from Dixie McNeil.

In the Second Division Kevin Sheedy made just 3 substitute appearances, against Fulham, Charlton Athletic and Nottingham Forest, until 23 March 1977, when he was selected for the starting line-up again. United drew 2-2 against Sheffield United, Steve Davey and Roy Carter scoring the goals for the Bulls, and Kevin Sheedy retained his place for the rest of the season, making 13 full appearances. He scored his first ever goal against Millwall at Edgar Street in a 3-1 win on 20 April 1977, with Dixie McNeil scoring a goal either side. Alexander was the goal scorer for Millwall. With the return of Steve Emery at right-back after injury, many felt that it was down to him and Sheedy that United started to win matches. The Bulls only lost three matches in which both the players started, beating Oldham, Milwall, Blackburn and Southampton.

His second goal came the following season when he made 24 League appearances for the Bulls. It came in a match against Carlisle United, which was a battle between two of the previous season's relegated clubs, when he scored the

Kevin Sheedy in action.

winner, a victory that lifted United off of the foot of the Third Division. Kevin made a total of 47 League appearances for Hereford United, scoring 4 goals.

After two years, during which he made fantastic progress, Kevin was transferred to Liverpool for an £80,000 fee in July 1978, but only made 3 Football League appearances for them in his four-year stay at Anfield. Realising his first-team options were limited at Liverpool he made the short journey across Stanley Park, transferring to Everton in August 1982 for £100,000, where he made an immediate impact. He became recognised as one of the best players in the First Division with his famous left foot. Kevin made 274 League appearances for Everton, scoring 67 times. Everton were League champions in 1984/85 and 1986/87, and were runners-up in the season in between. They were FA Cup winners in 1984 and runners-up in 1986 and 1989, and Football League Cup winners in 1984. Kevin played in over 40 internationals after first being capped in 1983, and featured in many of the Republic of Ireland's World Cup campaigns. His first full international appearance was as a substitute in a European Nations Cup game against Holland in October 1983. Ireland threw away a 2-0 lead in front of their home crowd in Dublin to lose 3-2. The following month he made the starting line-up against Malta, again in the European Nations Cup, and Sheedy scored his first international goal in an 8-0 victory. Lawrenson and Brady both scored two goals each, Stapleton, O'Callaghan and Daly scoring the others. One of his favourite goals was the one he scored against England in the 1990 World Cup, the match ending in a 1-1 draw. He later moved to St James' Park, home of Newcastle United, before moving on to Blackpool, eventually making well over 400 League appearances.

Peter Spiring

Midfield, 1976–1983

Football League era

	Appearances	Goals
League	205 (22)	20
Other	26 (1)	3

Previous clubs: Bristol City, Liverpool, Luton Town

Midfielder Peter Spiring joined Hereford United in February 1976. The Bulls had wanted to sign him earlier but Luton's price had been too high. Peter was born in Glastonbury, Somerset, in December 1950 and was originally on the books of Bristol City. He made 62 appearances for the Robins, scoring 16 goals, and was a former England youth international. The Ashton Gate club reached the semi-final of the Football League Cup when Peter was with them, when he had the privilege of playing against Tottenham Hotspur. Peter was then transferred to Liverpool in March 1973 but he did not make the grade, failing to make any first-team appearances. Moving on to Luton Town in 1974, he represented the Hatters on 12 occasions, scoring 2 goals. Arguably the most successful and enjoyable time of his career was at Hereford United between 1976 and 1982. During his time with the Bulls he made 205 appearances, scoring 20 goals. During his first season at Edgar Street Peter made 5 appearances, plus 1 as substitute. He made his debut on 7 February 1976 away at Mansfield Town while on loan from Luton. Coming on as a substitute, his goal-bound header came off the bar, allowing Dixie McNeil to score, the game ending in a 2-2 draw. His final League appearance of the season was in the 3-1 home victory over Preston North End in April 1976. The season ended in a farce, however, with Hereford United reaching the final of the Welsh Cup. The first leg was played at Cardiff but the clubs were ordered to replay it because Peter, who had played in the match, was ruled to be ineligible over confusion surrounding his earlier loan spell from Luton. There had been no complaints from Cardiff City and the first match ended in a 2-2 draw, with Peter scoring both goals for Hereford United. The first leg was ordered to be replayed at Hereford on 18 May and resulted in a 3-3 draw, with the second leg taking place at Ninian Park the next day and ending in a 2-3 defeat. What should have been an exciting end of season turned out to be damp squib, as the matches were arranged in such haste that many of the supporters of both clubs were not aware of the dates until afterwards. Cardiff City's manager did not even attend the second leg match at Ninian Park, preferring to play golf in Scotland! Playing Second Division football with the Bulls in the 1976/77 season Spiring made 36 full appearances and scored 10 goals. His first League goal for the club came in an away fixture against Nottingham Forest on 11 September 1975, Hereford finally losing 4-3. He hit a superb volley into the back of the net to give Hereford United a 2-0 lead, but their defence lost concentration and allowed Forest to go 4-2 up before the Bulls reduced the arrears. A week later Peter was on the scoresheet again as United drew with Carlisle United at Edgar Street. Peter was a regular member of the first team over the next few seasons, scoring some memorable goals, one of which was in the 6-1 win over Crewe Alexandra in the 1978/79 season. He had come on as a substitute for the injured John Layton and hit a twenty-five-yard shot that was blocked on the line, but with seven minutes remaining hit an even harder drive from further out that flashed under the bar.

After being a regular member of the Bulls' side for seven seasons 'Spiro', as he was known, played his last match for Hereford United at home against Peterborough United on 14 May 1983, which ended in a 1-0 defeat for the Edgar Street club. He was a consistent player who contributed a lot to the team. After he gave up playing football Peter established a business in Hereford as an electrician.

Chairman Frank Miles shakes hands with Peter Spiring while manager Sillett looks on.

Colin Tavener

Midfield, 1972–1974

Football League era

	Appearances	Goals
League	50 (1)	3
Other	5	

Previous clubs: Bath City, Trowbridge Town

Colin Tavener joined Hereford United prior to the start of the 1972/73 season for a £500 fee and proved to be a bargain buy. He had been born in Bath in June 1945 and had a short spell with Bath City before joining Trowbridge Town, where he stayed for nine years and made over 450 first-team appearances. Reports of his skills in midfield had reached Hereford United a few seasons earlier but Colin had been reluctant to move to another non-League club. When the chance came for him to join United during their time in the Fourth Division, Colin jumped at it. One of the many signings made by player-manager Colin Addison, Tavener made his League debut for the club at home to Aldershot on 25 November 1972 in a 1-0 win, after playing consistently well for the club's West Midlands team. Taking the place of the manager, who had broken his leg and was out for the rest of the season, Colin soon settled down in midfield, partnering David Rudge and Harry Gregory. The chance for full-time football had come perhaps a bit late for Colin and, now commanding a first-team place, he grasped the opportunity. He grew in confidence as he established himself as one of Hereford United's top players. No doubt he will never forget his first League goal for the club, which came on 27 January 1973. This was in a home fixture against Lincoln City, managed by one Graham Taylor who later became manager of England. Due to an injury crisis Taylor was forced to come out of retirement to play in a match that ended in a 2-1 for Hereford. Colin's first goal for the club came in the forty-fifth minute with Billy Tucker adding a second for a 2-0 lead. Hereford later earned a penalty that Lincoln goalkeeper John Kennedy saved, the spot-kick being taken by Colin Tavener. Then, to cap perhaps one of the most remarkable days in his footballing career, Colin managed to score an own goal in the sixty-ninth minute. At the end of the season Colin had made 28 full appearances for Hereford United plus 1 as substitute, scoring 1 goal. For all the players in the squad the joy of promotion at the first attempt to the Third Division was experienced on Saturday 28 April 1973 with the home victory over Crewe Alexandra. Colin always felt that he could do well if he was given a chance to play in the Football League and, when United came runners-up in the Fourth Division, he said, 'Now we have won promotion I just cannot describe my feelings, but I am sure that we will do well in the Third Division.'

On 25 August 1973 Hereford United made their debut in the Third Division in an away fixture at Grimsby Town. Colin Tavener scored the first goal for the club in that division in the seventy-third minute. The match ended in a 3-1 victory for United, a very good start in uncharted waters. After a 1-1 draw away to Halifax Town on 29 September 1973 Colin missed a number of matches for the club. He returned on 24 October 1973 in a home fixture against the League leaders Bristol Rovers. The game ended in a 0-0 draw before a crowd of 12,501. During the season Colin made 26 appearances in all for the club, scoring another goal against Blackburn Rovers on 1 January 1974. He played in both FA Cup fixtures against West Ham United that season, thus experiencing the cup glory that some of his teammates had already felt in the past. He departed the club at the end of the season, no doubt with fond memories of his time at Hereford United. He re-signed for Bath City, for whom he went on to make over 300 appearances. He also had a spell as player-manager at Twerton Park and played in both legs of the 1979 Southern League Cup final, when Bath beat Yeovil 1-0 on aggregate. While the name of Colin Tavener is not the most remembered or well known by Hereford United fans Colin played his part in two of the most exciting seasons in the club's history.

Colin Tavener in action.

Charlie Thompson

Striker, 1947–1958

Prior to 1972/73

	Appearances	Goals
League	452	184

Previous clubs: Bolsover Colliery, Sheffield United

Charlie Thompson will be fondly remembered by many Hereford United supporters for his famous goals and power as a centre forward. During his spell at Edgar Street he helped himself to quite a few club records, and indeed helped his team to break a few, Charlie was the idol of Edgar Street in the 1950s. He started playing football at the age of eight for his school team and then went on to play for the Doe Lea Valley Boys, a Derbyshire team. Charlie then went to work in the Midland Coalfields and played football for Bolsover Colliery, where he started to make a name for himself. They played in the Sheffield Association League and recorded wins of 12-1 against Stocksbridge and 7-0 against Lopham, when Thompson gave a classic display of ball control and shooting power. He scored five in his first match and six against Lopham. Against Sheffield University Charlie scored six goals. At the age of fifteen he joined the ground staff at Bramall Lane, the home of Sheffield United, and signed professional forms at the age of seventeen. He spent two years in the 'A' team, of which he became captain and, at the beginning of 1939, he was centre forward for the Sheffield United first team. A newspaper cutting of that time told how Sheffield beat Lincoln 9-0 and Charlie Thompson scored four goals: 'Sheffield's forwards passed through Lincoln's half-back and back divisions like water through a sieve.'

He made his name playing for Chesterfield and Sheffield United and had been tipped for international honours with England in 1940, but his hopes were dashed when he broke his leg badly at Villa Park in 1944. During the 1939-1944 period Charlie returned to the Bolsover Colliery before joining the RAF in 1943. He was stationed in Herefordshire but could always command his position in the Sheffield United team provided his duties allowed him to. Charlie was well known and respected for the number of miles he used to cycle or walk to make sure he caught his train to Sheffield on a Friday night, often arriving in the early hours of Saturday morning. Then, in the early hours of Sunday morning, he had to cycle the thirty-five miles back again. He first played at Edgar Street as a guest for Hereford United in the 1945/46 season while serving in the RAF. They won the Southern League Championship that year but were denied the title when points were awarded

Thompson shoots while playing for Hereford, *c.* 1950.

to Chelmsford City for the games that they were unable to play. The Bulls were known as 'the Lilywhites' then, despite having to change to black shorts in 1946. Charlie Thompson signed for Hereford United in the summer of 1947, at the same time as Jimmy Duggan and George Tranter had been transferred from West Bromwich Albion. Sheffield United were reluctant to let him go but he wanted to retire from League football and as he was so popular they did not feel they could stand in his way. In his last season with them he had played in six different positions, so great was his versatility. In the next eleven years with Hereford United, Charlie scored 184 goals in 452 first-team appearances, a club record at that time. He will remain a hero in the eyes of many United supporters as he was everyone's idol. There are a number of supporters who think he was the most memorable player ever to play for Hereford. He was a traditional English centre forward, tall and fearless. His agility and shooting power plus his physique made him a match for any defence. This razor-sharp eye for goal inside the penalty area and his knowledge of the game, plus his ability to know where his fellow teammates were, made him a fantastic team player. Few centre halves could beat him in the air and his tactics were always scrupulously fair. He had learnt his football thoroughly, not only the practical side but the theory too. Charlie was popular with his teammates and always put his team first in everything that he did. He was an instant success, scoring a hat-trick in his first home match in the 1947/48 season against Gravesend. Thynnes Athletic were drawn against Hereford United in the preliminary round of the FA Cup, much to the regret of their goalkeeper after he was on the wrong end of an 11-0 defeat. Eight of the goals were scored by United's hero, an individual goal-scoring record that is unlikely to be beaten. Woods, the Thynnes goalkeeper, broke his wrist making a superb save from a cracking, powerful shot from Charlie. The 11-0 victory was also a club record in competitive football. However, Hereford United did not get beyond the second qualifying round, for after beating Stafford 2-1 they slumped to a 4-0 defeat at Stourbridge. In early December, United were top of the league following 5-0 and 5-2 wins against Torquay Reserves and Yeovil. Jimmy Duggan scored hat-tricks in both matches, having signed from West Bromwich Albion at the same time as Charlie. Just after Christmas Merthyr Tydfil were the visitors and United were second in the league. A record crowd of 7,000 paid £506 to watch the match, which ended in a goal-less draw. The team from Wales went on to win the league by six points from Gillingham with United finishing fifth with 42 points, having won 16 matches and scored 77 goals. The biggest wins were 7-1 against Cheltenham and 6-1 against Guildford, but they were beaten 8-1 in a Southern League Cup match away at Merthyr. Charlie continued to score fantastic goals for United and in the 1948/49 season in the Southern League he scored five against Guildford. In the same season he scored United's first ever goal in the FA Cup second round, against Exeter City. During the 1955/56 season Nuneaton Borough were on the receiving end of an 8-1 defeat, Charlie scoring four of the goals. He also scored numerous hat-tricks in the Southern League and FA Cup. When a benefit match was arranged for Charlie Thompson in 1950, 8,000 supporters watched United play a League XI, such was his popularity. The arrival of Tommy Best at Edgar Street in the summer of 1950 led to Charlie switching to centre half, but he continued to dominate the matches and scored many more goals. In the summer of 1955 Charlie Thompson was forced into retirement from playing football because of an eye injury sustained in a match. This was a terrible blow for the club but such was his spirit that, when the club started to get into difficulties, he went to the board and told them he would start playing again and would not hold the club responsible if playing made his injury worse. He was back in action in October 1955 after first leading the reserves, and he scored four goals in his comeback match against Nuneaton Borough. Another benefit match was held for Charlie Thompson at Edgar Street in March 1958 when Sheffield United were the opposition. He eventually retired from playing football in 1958 but continued to help the club in a number of other ways. He became assistant manager, trainer, scout, bus driver and pools organiser before finishing as a radio commentator for the local Radio Lions hospital broadcasts from Edgar Street. His knowledge of the beautiful game continued to aid Hereford United for a long time after he stopped dazzling defences on the football pitch and he helped coach many youngsters in the Hereford area. He sadly died after a long illness in August 1997 in Hereford on the day that Hereford United played at Penydarren Park, the home of Merthyr Tydfil, a team that Charlie Thompson had played against many times for Hereford United. There had never been a more popular player at Edgar Street; old and young, male and female supporters all loved him and his sportmanship. His playing ability and loyalty to the club had won him many friends. The chairman of the time, Peter Hill, called Charlie Thompson one of the all-time greats of Hereford United.

Peter Timms

Defender, 1962–1971

Prior to 1972/73

	Appearances	Goals
	305	

Peter Timms made over 300 first-team appearances for Hereford United, following in the footsteps of Charlie Thompson, Johnny Layton, Roy Williams, Reggie Bowen and Ray Daniel. A determined defender, Peter gained the support of all the Bulls' fans and was a popular member of the team during the 1960s. He started out as an inside forward before being converted into a left-back.

Peter was born at Smethwick and soon caught the eye as a promising player when a pupil at James Watt Technical College. When he left school Peter played in the Birmingham Coronation League and then joined the Springers, who competed in the Birmingham Youth and Old Boys League. During his first season with the club they finished runners-up and the second year they went one better by winning the League. At this time Peter was playing as an amateur inside forward and putting in some impressive displays.

In 1960 Peter moved to Hereford and soon started to make a name for himself with his performances in the Herefordshire League, playing for Wiggins. As a result he was invited to join Hereford United in 1962 and, during the 1962/63 season, he made 6 appearances for the reserve team. Bob Dennison took over as manager from Ray Daniel, after having managed Middlesbrough and Northampton Town, in December 1963 and a new era started for Peter. He was promptly given a game in the first team against Dudley in the Worcestershire Senior Cup and a month later he made his debut for United in the Southern League in an away match at Rugby. Peter only made one more appearance for the Bulls that season, but the following season Bob Dennison decided to try Peter as a left-back, with great success. A few weeks later he was signed on professional terms and he did not miss one of the club's remaining fifty-three games that season. He played a prominent role in Hereford United's championship success, which took them back into the Premier Division. Peter also had the distinction of scoring the team's 100th League goal in the closing weeks of the season, and this also happened to be Peter's first goal for the senior team.

Peter Timms

Defender, 1962–1971

Peter was a regular member of the first team for the next three seasons, making 51 appearances in 1965/66, 45 the following season and 49 the next. In 1968/69 Peter was only able to make 28 appearances but in 1969/70 the tally was back up to 55. During the 1970/71 season Peter made his 300th first-team appearance in a Welsh Cup match against Merthyr Tydfil, and went on to make 22 more appearances. Sadly he was injured playing against Yeovil a week before the semi-final of the FA Trophy and was forced to miss the match against Hillingdon Borough. In recognition of the vast contribution Peter made to the club he was awarded a benefit match, when Fulham were invited to Edgar Street on 12 May 1971. They honoured Peter by bringing their first team, who a fortnight earlier had won promotion to the Second Division. A total of 3,560 fans came to the match, and this proved to be Peter's last game for Hereford United. He shared in many of Hereford United's triumphs, including a match against Third Division Millwall, who United beat 1-0 courtesy of a goal from Ron Fogg in 1965/66. Millwall were ten points clear in the Third Division and went on to promotion. Their goalkeeper was none other than Alex Stepney. The following Monday Peter went to work and he and his mates sat around the radio, listening to the draw, but there was great disappointment when Bedford Town came out of the hat. One of Peter's fondest memories is of reaching the Welsh Cup final for the first time in United's history, after beating Newport County. The day after the cup final Peter flew out to Rhodesia (now known as Zimbabwe) as a member of the John Charles XI who went on tour, playing a total of fourteen games.

Peter's determined tackling, coupled with his speed and skill, made him a natural defender and he always enjoyed a high degree of popularity with Hereford United supporters. He also played in the local teams Wiggins and Lads Club before retiring in 1978. He had the pleasure of playing with some great players; in one game against Kidderminster Harriers Peter lined up with John Charles, Eddie Holliday and Ray Daniel, all ex-internationals. They had drawn the first match in the FA Cup at Edgar Street, and in the replay Kidderminster were allowed to take the lead. At half-time there was silence in the dressing room apart from Ray Daniel and Peter Timms arguing, blaming each other for the goal! In the second half the three internationals were brilliant, as well as Peter, and the team won 4-2. At the end of the game Peter tried to apologise to Ray and to the manager Bob Dennison for what had been said in the dressing room. Bob replied, 'Don't apologise, you can have a row every week if you come out and play like that after. Preferably have the argument before you start the match!'

Billy Tucker

Defender, 1971–1977

Prior to 1972/73

	Appearances	Goals
	45	

Football League era

	Appearances	Goals
League	135 (2)	12
Other	9 (1)	2

Previous clubs: Kidderminster Harriers, Evesham United

Billy Tucker, another of the Giant-killing team, was born in Kidderminster on 17 May 1948. He was a defender who represented his county, Worcestershire, at amateur level. He was originally on the books of Kidderminster Harriers and played over 100 games for their reserves. Billy then moved to Evesham United, who played in the Midland Combination. It was while playing against Hereford United in the Worcestershire Senior Cup that Billy Tucker came up against John Charles, and he made such a good job of marking him out of the game that the Bulls' manager immediately took steps to sign him on for Hereford United. He did not sign on as a professional player as he continued to further his main occupation as a bank clerk.

In September 1971 he made his debut in the Southern League for United but it was not until the FA Cup that Billy Tucker made a big impression. It was in a 5-0 win over one of his former clubs, Kidderminster Harriers. Most fans remember Billy Tucker for his power in the air; his clearances from opponents' attacks and goal-bound headers from corners were brilliant. He had a wonderful sense of timing and positional play, even if his style looked awkward. He helped the Bulls to many victories, all of which helped the Edgar Street football club to achieve its goal of Football League status in 1972. In March 1972 the fans feared that Hereford United would lose one of its favourite players when a press report told of an approach from a South African First Division club. However, the success of the Giant-killing team and the lure of playing in the Football League was enough to persuade Billy to sign professional forms and stay at Edgar Street.

He continued at the heart of United's defence and Fourth Division forwards found it difficult to get past Billy Tucker, especially when the opposition had been awarded corners. His ability to jump inches above his opponents and the power of his headers proved to be memorable and he also scored some important goals for United in the Fourth Division promotion season of 1972/73. Billy Tucker had made himself very popular with the Edgar Street faithful and he was voted the Player of the Year in 1972/73. He had scored 8 goals in 42 League appearances for

Billy Tucker

Defender, 1971–1977

Tucker wins the ball.

the Bulls. One goal was scored on a very foggy day against Colchester when the fans down one end had to shout to those down at the other end to tell them who had scored! At the end of the final match of the 1972/73 season the jubilant Hereford United fans invaded the Edgar Street pitch. Most of the players had already reached the dressing room – except, that is, for Billy Tucker. The supporters ignored any health and safety regulations and lifted Billy shoulder-high. A concerned PA announcer begged them 'Be careful with him boys, we will need him next year in the Third Division.' The following two seasons he only scored one League goal in each season in 36 and 35 appearances. Billy also achieved the distinction of being the first player to play 100 Football League games in Hereford United's colours. He was the hero in the FA Cup match at home to Gillingham in November 1974 when he scored the only goal of the game, a first-class header from a cross by Terry Paine. United's reward was an away tie to Cambridge United where they were beaten 2-0. It was only the third time in quarter of a century that they were beaten by lower-graded opposition. With the arrival of new faces at Edgar Street, in particular John Galley and John Layton, Billy's appearances the following season went down to just 17, but he did score 3 goals. One of the goals was scored in the FA Cup at home against Torquay United, which made sure of victory and gave United the chance to play Bournemouth in the next round. The two League goals were against Preston North End and Sheffield Wednesday. Billy Tucker joined Bury permanently in January 1977 after joining them on loan in December 1976. At Gigg Lane he scored 8 goals and made 96 appearances for Bury before being transferred to Swindon Town in 1979. Swindon Town were a Third Division side at the time and Billy Tucker scored 4 goals in 35 matches. One of these goals was against his former side Bury when his new team beat the side from Gigg Lane 8-0. Other achievements with Swindon Town include two good cup runs and playing in the semi-final of the Football League Cup. Billy Tucker went on to play for non-League Cheltenham Town, a team that he also helped out as a coach. On the few occasions when Billy returned to Edgar Street while playing for the opposition, he was given a very warm welcome by the Hereford United fans, such was their respect for him.

Billy Tucker with the Player of the Year trophy.

Dudley Tyler

Midfield, 1969–1972, 1973–1976

Prior to 1972/73

	Appearances	Goals
	116	

Football League era

	Appearances	Goals
League	97 (5)	10
Other	13 (1)	2

Previous clubs: Pinehurst, West Ham United

Dudley Tyler was a midfield player who loved playing out on the wing, and he joined Hereford United as an amateur in August 1969, juggling football with being a cost accountant. Dudley was voted Player of the Year in 1970, such was his popularity with the Edgar Street faithful, and he scored 60 goals in over 300 first-team appearances. Hereford United fans enjoyed his forays on the outskirts of the pitch and many goals came as a result of his inch-perfect crosses. He became known as 'Cuddly Dudley' by some of his admirers!

He was a member of the club's successful non-League FA Cup team that reached the fourth round of the cup before being sold to West Ham United for £25,000 in July 1972. After 29 appearances for the Hammers he returned to Edgar Street for a £15,000 fee in November 1973.

Dudley Tyler was born in Salisbury in September 1944 and he was twenty-four when he was invited to play in Hereford United's pre-season trial matches prior to the commencement of the 1969/70 Southern League campaign. He very nearly did not make it to Edgar Street in time, as a friend who had offered to bring Dudley to the ground was delayed and he did not arrive until 7.25 p.m. Luckily the opposition was also delayed, the coach bringing Brereton Sports for a West Midlands League match broke down, and they did not arrive until 8.30 p.m. At the time Dudley played (for eight seasons) in the Hellenic League for Pinehurst, a local side who played just outside Swindon, starting as a junior. During his spell as a junior he won 10 county caps for Wiltshire. He had tried but failed to break into League football, having had trials with Reading, Swindon and Luton Town. Perhaps the fact that he had a hole-in-the-heart operation at the age of fifteen deterred League managers from pursuing their initial interest. However, the Hereford United manager John Charles took the gamble and Dudley Tyler soon became a favourite with the fans. He became an important member of a very strong Southern League side, leaving defenders mesmerised by his skill and speed down the wing. He signed professional forms after only three games with United and scored

Dudley Tyler

Midfield, 1969–1972, 1973–1976

Tyler in action, *c.* 1975.

21 goals in his first season. His ability to turn defenders and speed down the line brought the League scouts to Edgar Street, many attacks and goals coming from his expertise. Hereford United turned down an offer of £5,000 from Fulham during Dudley's first season with them, as the manager felt that he was worth more than that. Dudley scored the winning goal at The Hawthorns against Northampton Town on a cold, wet night. Billy Meadows knocked the ball in and it was a three-way race between Dudley, Phil Neal (who went on to play for Liverpool), and their goalkeeper. Fortunately Dudley got to the ball first and knocked it into the empty net from the edge of the box. Dudley ended up on his back in the mud as the crowd went wild; he later said he had never known so much noise! His displays against both Newcastle United and West Ham in the FA Cup run earned him a move to Upton Park for a fee of £25,000 at the end of the season, a record for a non-League player in 1972. Watching Dudley in action against West Ham, their manager Ron Greenwood saw his potential and invited him to play in a testimonial match for Millwall's Harry Cripps. Dudley scored two goals and soon signed for West Ham.

On the opening day of the 1972/73 season he lined up with England skipper Bobby Moore plus Billy Bonds and Trevor Brooking at The Hawthorns against West Bromwich Albion. Dudley Tyler scored one League goal for the Hammers, a memorable goal past Peter Shilton, but it was probably too late in his career to make a big impact in the First Division. On a return visit to Hereford, as a guest at the annual dinner and dance at Wormelow, Dudley told everyone how the first result that he looked for on a Saturday was that of Hereford United. He made 21 appearances in the First Division in his first season and 8 the following season. Unfortunately Dudley suffered a broken collarbone in his first season at Upton Park, and struggled to get into the first team in his second season there. He played several games for their reserves at the bottom of the Football Combination League but these matches attracted smaller crowds than Dudley had experienced at Edgar Street. Dudley had to play a more defensive game at Upton Park and tackle more, and he later confessed to being unhappy at West Ham. He felt isolated there; at Hereford everyone was part of the club, on and off the pitch, but he enjoyed the experience of playing for West Ham. He preferred the atmosphere at Edgar Street as the supporters really made him feel welcome. Once back in the Bulls' shirt he marked his return by opening the scoring in a 3-1 win over Walsall after a £15,000 fee had been agreed for his transfer in November 1973. Hinch and Evans were the other two goal scorers. A month later he was back at Upton Park playing for United against West Ham in the FA Cup, and his performance led the Hammers' fans to wonder why he had been let go as United drew 1-1 and then won the replay 2-1. Towards the end of the season Dudley broke his ankle in a home match against Southport, but he was fit for the start of the 1975/76 season and United went on to win the Third Division title, Dudley scoring 5 League goals. Dudley remained with the Bulls for three seasons, making over 300 appearances for the club. He linked well with Terry Paine, Steve Davey and Dixie McNeil, and said that it was the wonderful team spirit that existed among the players at Edgar Street that helped them achieve so much in the FA Cup and win the Third Division. In 97 League appearances he scored 10 goals. He was the last member of the Giant-killing squad to leave Edgar Street. He was advised to give up full-time football in December 1976 due to a persistent ankle injury and returned to the non-League, playing for Malvern Town and Pegasus. In 1980 he was appointed manager of Malvern Town and he has also coached a Tupsley Pegasus League side. A very popular player for United, Dudley Tyler has remained living in Hereford and has attended various reunions of the Giant-killing team. The Giant-killers turned out in force for Dudley's testimonial game and followed tradition by having a steak meal at the Spread Eagle and a pre-match conference at the Green Dragon before walking to the ground. John Sillett paid tribute to Dudley by saying: 'Dudley has always been the type of player that every manager wants in his side. His tremendous pace, ball control and skill was a great asset to the team, and it was a big blow when we learned that he had to give up full-time football. Dudley was a player who could pick up a ball deep inside our half and change the course of the game; he could get around the back of defences and turn defeat into victory with a flash of genius. When he was song there was no-one to rival him.'

Dudley Tyler has just scored for Hereford at Edgar Street, *c.* 1974.

Joe Wade

Defender, 1956–1962

Prior to 1972//73

	Appearances	Goals
	134	

Previous clubs: Arsenal

Once described as an absolute gentleman, Joe Wade joined Hereford United in 1956, a stylish full-back from Arsenal. Joe was born in London and joined Arsenal as an amateur in 1944, spending over ten years at Highbury after signing professional forms in 1945. It was not until the 1952/53 season that he became a first-team regular, winning a First Division championship medal during his first full season, playing in 40 of the club's 42 League games, pipping Preston North End on goal average for the championship. He was well known for his burst of speed: 'there can be few faster backs in the game' was a quote of the time. He was selected for the Football League representative team while at Highbury. He was captain of Arsenal and played in the same side as Joe Mercer, and had the unfortunate distinction of being the man who finished Mercer's career. A collision during a First Division match at Highbury resulted in a broken leg for the wing half.

One big disappointment for Joe whilst playing for the Gunners was that they did not reach the final of the FA Cup in 1953, losing out to Blackpool. Arsenal had been tipped to win the double, and they were setting the pace in the First Division. They had beaten Burnley and were drawn at home to Blackpool in the quarter-finals. The Arsenal team, which also included another Hereford United great, Welsh international centre half Ray Daniel, were beaten 2-1 by a Blackpool team that included Stanley Matthews. In the semi-finals Blackpool pipped Tottenham Hotspur 2-1 and then beat Bolton Wanderers 4-3 in an epic Wembley final. It was almost twenty years later before Arsenal eventually achieved the League and cup double in 1971.

Joe played as a guest for Hereford United during the war years and joined United in 1956 as player-manager for an undisclosed fee. The late Fred Turner, Hereford United's secretary, stated that it was obvious that Arsenal would ask a transfer fee, otherwise they would have every non-League club pestering them for player-managers. The Gunners agreed to play at Edgar Street as part of the deal and a gate of nearly 7,000 helped recoup some of the transfer fee, the Gunners winning the match

4-0. Earlier in the day the Queen and Duke of Edinburgh had toured the county and part of their itinerary was a visit to the Edgar Street ground, where thousands of school children packed the terraces to cheer the royal couple. Joe Wade's drive and enthusiasm at left-back earned him two Southern League Cup medals and United reached the third round of the FA Cup for the first time in their history. He made a total of 134 appearances for United and during that time United won the League Charity Shield and the North-West title before being beaten by Bedford Town in a play-off match for the championship. In 1958 he was voted Hereford's Sportsman of the Year, his popularity making him an obvious choice. Joe Wade and Charlie Thompson adapted an amazing training strategy at Edgar Street, and it was down to their foresight that Ronnie Clayton and Freddie Jones were transferred to Arsenal for a combined fee of £5,000. They had come to the attention of the bigger clubs after the FA Cup match against Sheffield Wednesday. Hereford United's incredible 6-1 victory over Queens Park Rangers when they had visited Edgar Street in 1957/58 had put them into the third round for the first time. It was the biggest win by a non-League club side over Football League opposition in history. A record attendance of 18,114 saw the match against Sheffield. The fans stood wherever there was an inch of space; hand grenade boxes were bought in from the local munitions factory. There were no health and safety rules in force then and no announcements from the PA system concerning not standing in restricted areas. Sheffield Wednesday won 3-0, but it was a hard-fought victory with Sheffield scoring two late goals.

Hereford United produced one of their greatest victories as a non-League club when they beat Cardiff City at Ninian Park. The Bluebirds were a Second Division side at the time. It was in a fifth-round tie of the Welsh Cup in 1958 and was described as one of the best results in the history of the club. It was the club's first ever victory over a Second Division side in competitive football and a first ever away win over a League club. Cardiff had indeed been strengthened by the return of ex-internationals Ray Daniel and Derrick Sullivan, who had been out since the previous November. Only 2,631 people saw the match, including a lively group of fans from Hereford, who yelled themselves hoarse cheering their team on to victory. Cardiff City had still not installed floodlights and rejected Hereford United's suggestion that the game could be played at Edgar Street under floodlights, opting instead to play the match at three o'clock on a Wednesday afternoon.

In 1961 there were further matches against League opposition; this time Bristol City were their opponents. The result at Ashton Gate was a 1-1 draw but sadly United lost the replay at Edgar Street 5-2. In 1962 Joe Wade resigned from Hereford United. He had opened a sports shop in Commercial Road, Hereford, and decided to devote more time to this successful enterprise.

Joe died after a short illness at the age of eighty-four in November 2005.

Steve White

Striker, 1994–1996

Football League era

	Appearances	Goals
League	70 (6)	44
Other	11	6

Previous clubs: Mangotsfield, Bristol Rovers, Luton Town, Charlton Athletic, Swindon Town

Steve James White was born in Chipping Sodbury in January 1959. He was a schoolboy international who had spells with Frampton Rangers and Mangotsfield United, before joining Bristol Rovers in July 1977, for whom he scored on his home debut in a 4-1 win over Sheffield United in April 1978. His great goal-scoring ratio per game attracted much attention. He scored 24 goals in 55 League and cup games for the Pirates before moving to Luton Town for a record £200,000 in December 1979. During his spell at Kenilworth Road Steve scored four goals in one game against Grimsby Town and helped them to win promotion to the First Division. He had scored 26 goals in 72 matches by the time he moved to Charlton Athletic in July 1982 for £150,000. During the season Steve White spent at The Valley he went out on loan to Lincoln City and Luton Town before moving back to Bristol Rovers in August 1983 for £45,000. Financial problems led to his move to Swindon Town in July 1986, Lou Macari signing Steve on a free transfer. It proved to be one of Town's best ever signings, as Steve went on to become one of the club's most prolific goal-scorers, was influential in much of the Robins' success during the 1980s and early 1990s. He remembers: 'We had so much success here. I was lucky enough to play at Wembley twice, and also under three magnificent managers.' Steve describes some of his best moments in football as being the matches he played at Wembley in 1990 and 1993, being on the winning side both times. His 18 goals for Swindon in the 1989/90 season helped them to a First Division place that in fact they were deprived of for alleged financial irregularities. Steve spent eight years at the County Ground as a player. Eventually, in 1993/94, he did play in the top flight after another promotion run, scoring 7 goals. Before bringing his Swindon Town career to a close in 1994 he had chalked up 111 goals in just over 250 appearances in the red and white, thus earning him a place in many Swindon Town fans' hearts, and he was rewarded with a benefit match in August 1992.

Goalscorer supreme White shoots for goal in 1995/96. The play-offs beckon.

However, Steve's goal scoring exploits did not end there. Between 1994 and 1996 he continued his goal every other game ratio, scoring 52 times in just under 100 appearances for Hereford, who he had joined on a free transfer in the summer of 1994. During that time he again endeared himself to the home fans and helped the club to its highest point. His first match for United was against Walsall at home, which ended in a goal-less draw. The fans only had to wait a week for his first goal, which was scored away to Rochdale in a 3-1 victory, Preedy and James scoring the other two goals. A week later Steve scored his first goal at Edgar Street at home to Wigan Athletic, but United threw away the three points, losing 2-1. 'Chalky', as Steve was nicknamed, returned to the County Ground at Swindon while with Hereford United, scoring a memorable winner to take United through to the Auto Windscreens Shield Southern Section quarter-final. He then scored twice in the second round of the FA Cup, latching on to crosses from Kevin Lloyd and then Richard Wilkins against Sutton United, to set up a third-round match against Tottenham Hotspur.

In the 1995/96 season Steve was Hereford United's top goal scorer with 34 goals. Not since the 1970s had Hereford United supporters seen such a prolific goal scorer, and he was rewarded by the fans, who awarded him the Player of the Year trophy. He scored a hat-trick in the 3-0 win over promotion rivals Plymouth Argyle. Steve White was the highest scorer in the Football League, scoring 29 goals in 40

League appearances. This was a remarkable feat at the age of thirty-seven. He has described one of the worst moments in his footballing career as being when Hereford United lost in the semi-final play-off against Darlington. The Bulls fans were sorry to see Steve leave and go to Cardiff City, but he was offered a two-year contract by the Bluebirds and Graham Turner had inherited a club with financial problems. The United manager unfortunately needed to cut the wage bill.

With such an abundance of experience it is little surprise that Steve used his talents in a managerial capacity, working alongside another former Swindon Town hero, Paul Bodin, at Bath City. He then went on to manage Chippenham Town.

Other titles published by Tempus

Hereford United Football Club

DENISE POWELL & DAVE EDGE

During the last 35 years at Edgar Street, the home of Hereford United Football Club, there have been some amazing FA Cup victories, a Welsh Cup win, a championship triumph and, of course, the ultimate relegation from the Football League. All of these epic events are covered by this book.

0 7524 3155 2

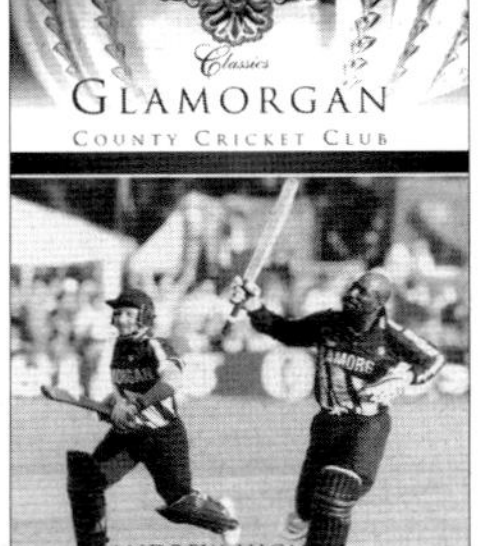

Glamorgan County Cricket Club Classics

ANDREW HIGNELL

This book traces the history of the club through fifty encounters that were particularly memorable, either for a great victory or a closely fought battle which ended in defeat. From Minor County matches at the end of the nineteenth century through to the triumphs of the year 2000, the games chosen can all be deemed 'classics'. Over 100 pictures have been chosen to illustrate these epic matches, showing key players, significant moments on the pitch and celebration.

0 7524 2182 4

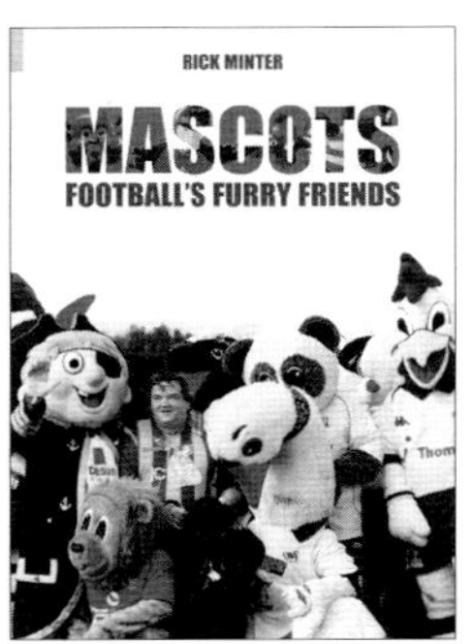

Mascots Football's Furry Friends

RICK MINTER

Meet the mascots in this remarkable illustrated guide. It reveals a crazy and colourful world of glamour, fun and rivalry, where football's pecking order works in reverse! The book includes a low-down on every mascot, with profiles of characters in the Premiership, Football League, Scotland and beyond.

0 7524 3179 X

Herefordshire Life

KEITH JAMES

Born in Herefordshire, photographer Derek Evans is one of a crop of distinguished photojournalists who recorded Britain through the mid-twentieth century and beyond. Illustrating some of the Herefordshire people and places he photographed around the mid-1950s, with images ranging from the cider factories to cigar-smoking Len Weston, chairman of the local football club, this book will delight those who know the area.

0 7524 3724 0

If you are interested in purchasing other books published by Tempus, or in case you have difficulty finding any Tempus books in your local bookshop, you can also place orders directly through our website

www.tempus-publishing.com